BE MORE BETTER:
STUFF TO KNOW AND USE

By:

Michael J. Czuchnicki

www.BeMoreBetterBooks.com

Be More Better: Stuff to Know and Use

by Michael J. Czuchnicki

Copyright © 2012 All rights reserved.

ISBN: 978-0-9883578-1-5

This book is also available as an e-book.

TABLE OF CONTENTS

ACKNOWLEDGEMENTS

This work was begun with my son, Anthony, in mind. Whatever it has evolved into is not his fault.

I would like to thank the many who read, commented on, or extended this work. I am indebted to them for their endless patience, kindness, knowledge, and most importantly, friendship. Those who helped include: my brother Eugene, Joseph Milano, Michael Benette, Paul Hennion...

... and of course, my darling Theresa.

INTRODUCTION

This is the first of the Be More Better Books series. It may add another to the pile of excellent self-help books – or it may be a real stinker. When you reach its end, you can tell us. You will quickly see if it is useful and enjoyable, so you won't waste a lot of valuable time.

Why read this book? What is in it for you?

Many business, military, and political leaders have written advice or self-help books. Some of their titles are wonderful, stressing: "Leadership," "Success," or "Secrets." Many use the "Lords of History" like Lincoln, or even Attila the Hun, to catch your eye. We don't.

This book really has Stuff to Know and Use, just as the title says.

The former are facts, understanding, and perspective that everyone should have at their fingertips. The latter are practical know-how and skills that you will need. You get both of these in short, digestible, and interesting bites. You will also get surprised, so be forewarned.

Success today, is often not about what you do, but rather what you know. Knowing that you *can* learn is the first step. Sadly, too many people believe themselves incapable of learning. By the end of this book, you will have no doubt of your abilities. You will have received much, and in such a way that it will stay with you. You can then use and benefit from it. None will be difficult; all is useful. When you become very interested in something, excellent! Dive deeper, later. Huge benefits come from the pool of knowledge.

There is a lot here on a practical level. Skills include: speaking and writing; analysis and planning; ordering and leading. There are also unusual and amusing view-points about the ever-changing technologies around you.

This is not a typical self-help book. There are no endless references. Question anything here and you will have made yourself better. The intention is not to answer everything but to give you tools to succeed. Plato said: "Knowledge is the food of the soul."

The Motivation Section highlights the importance of choosing. Then there are some mystery biographies. Who did they become? Something you don't know you know follows.

The Skills Section reviews some skills that should have been learned in school – or perhaps you just forgot. These are needed by everyone – you included. Even if you consider yourself an expert on some of them, we will make you better.

You get some science and technology. There are stories about some "Everyday Miracles." The mysteries of the computer will be exposed – an understanding that is essential. "The Internet's Origins" is a story you'll not forget – a guaranty.

The book ends with some essential facts. It is important to make mistakes as long as you know how to handle them. And finally, "You Are Smart" will give you a *Wow* as proof of this empowering idea.

You will have a rich feast in the pages to follow – but we hope you will finish hungry for more.

Chapter 1 – YOU CAN DANCE

If my parents had sent me to a New York City public high school, a pretty girl might have had the locker next to mine. That didn't happen. Mom and Dad sent me to a Catholic school. These keep the sexes miles apart during school hours to protect us from ourselves and to keep the faculty and administration out of any cross-fire.

When the last bell rang, there were many activities – sports, clubs, jobs, and even study to exhaust us students physically and mentally. It always seemed to have been a considered plan, even a plot. It still seems that way to me, even through the prism of time. However, there was one important exception to the separation of boys from girls – the Saturday night dance.

The Dance was feared by all underclass students, from the lowly Freshmen to the almost-as-low Sophomores. Equally traumatized were those suffering from acne, low self-confidence, a lack of coordination, and the many other teen afflictions. The Juniors welcomed the dances, but not as much as did the Seniors and their steadies. The dances were held in the gym. The weak-of-body considered this to be a school-week version of a medieval dungeon. But, for each dance, the cavernous space would become a different world. Each dance had a theme: "Across the Sea," "Knights and their Ladies," or "Under the Spring Stars." This guided the dance committee's work as they created a fairyland of dancing lights and glittering decorations.

The bleachers would be pushed back, folding onto themselves to form slotted, wood walls six-feet high. Everyone would pile their jackets on top. The imaginary world would be dimly lit. A rotating, faceted, mirrored

ball would dominate center-court, dazzling our eyes as it reflected the spotlights focused on it. The moving waves of the light-storm would reach out to the most distant corners of the gym.

There, horses rested, seemingly tethered to the hated parallel bars – indistinctly seen, but always lurking.

I was sixteen, a good student, and on the track team. You can see my priorities from that list. That my eyes were less than perfect is an understatement – my glasses were as thick as Coke-bottle bottoms. But that day, for whatever reason, I had decided the time was right for me to go to The Dance. Going alone was probably a mistake. Flying solo is an advanced skill, but scars are often earned the hard way – through stupidity. Still, I was excited, afraid, and very unsure of what to do. Dressing was an agony of indecision with repeated raids on my closet. Should I wear an undershirt? What about a tie? The daily commute to school was well-practiced: Take the Eighth Avenue bus to 69th Street and transfer. Because I had to wait outside at the bus-stop, Mama made me wear a jacket. It was autumn, and she did not want me to catch a cold; God bless her!

On arrival at my school, I got on the line to pay the nominal admission with money from my part-time job at the library. Beyond the ticket-table, noise poured through the thrown-wide double-doors. The echoing cacophony simultaneously enticed and amplified my fears. You could not hear yourself think – less so the closer you approached. It was wonderful, exhilarating, and frightening.

Entering the transformed gym for the first time, we *newbies* found ourselves confronted with something unlike anything ever experienced, so our natural instinct to seek protection took over. Most of us younger boys herded together at the back of the gym. There we were as far away as possible from the girls. They formed a gaggle in front, near the band. Down each side-line there were various boy-packs. There were the in-crowd groups, each believing theirs the best, and looking down at everyone else. The jocks were divided by their sport: basketball, track, or baseball. Even the nerds had their own distinct multiple assemblies: band and newspaper.

No-man's-land was the center of the hardwood floor, where basketball games were held on Friday nights. Later this same night, those highly-polished boards would be the scene of a different sort of game, frantic scrums between guys and their girls. The boys would be trying to go just one inch further; the young ladies would be resisting coyly. All the couples would be rushed, anticipating the chaperones' "Leave room for the Holy Ghost" remonstrance. These jokingly-serious words were always spoken with hands on the couples' shoulders pulling the inexperienced lovers apart during the slow dances.

All during the evening, the younger boys would periodically leave the pack to chase each other, stopping with long slides on leather-sole-dress-shoes. Others adopted a hanging-out posture as they lazily combed their unruly hair back into style – even as they secretly watched the girls. No matter what laughingly-transparent surveillance method we boys adopted, the young, fair maidens remained near, and yet so far. They were other-worldly. They were beautiful and alluring, but impossible to attain except by luck. We thought that the only way to get a girl was to have the *handsome gene*; or parents rich enough to provide a car...but, if you had neither, what then?

It turns out that there was an easy answer to this question. It was something in books, heard on the radio, and seen on TV. Even those who we looked up to most – real-life heroes – spoke about it, saying that though they were afraid, even terrified, they just did what the situation called for. If a hero could choose how to act in the face of a really big thing – like saving people from a burning building – anyone could do the same for a lesser thing. Here in the loud, dim gym, there were no fires visible – only those in our hearts. Perhaps it was the false feeling of being safe because of the darkness – certainly I cannot ever be accused of being brave – it might have been stupidity, but I decided to go and ask a girl to dance.

Walking across the gym's wooden floor was harder than expected. The problem was fear, certainly the journey was not physically demanding. That very morning, I'd competed in a 2.5 mile, cross-country race in Van Cortland Park. A lot of track teams were there. The starting-line stretched for 100 yards at the edge of a grassy field. At its other side was the dreaded cow-path, a 20 foot-wide rocky, dirt trail curving up and around the first, tall hill. The quarter-mile dash at the start of the race was feared. At best, you reached the hill out of breath, heart pounding, and in pain. The Pack, as the almost one-thousand athletes was known, was dangerous. Everyone was funneled into that narrow path. Elbows hit, feet entangled, and runners got knocked down. The lucky ones were hurdled by those behind; if not, they would find themselves at the bottom of a hot and sweaty pile. We all wore spikes – quarter-inch needles of steel on the soles of our track-shoes which left permanent scars when pounded into, or ripped through flesh – so falling was dangerous.

This morning's heart-pounding, out-of-breath, fear of danger was about the same feeling I had crossing the gym. The song playing had ended, and there was a short interval as the band – their name, still remembered, Crystal Dream – got coordinated for the next. In that interval, in the dimness, I had to choose someone to ask to dance. It was hard to do so as the girls all seemed out of focus, or so they seemed to me. I could hear the band-leader call to his group, so I knew it was now, or stand and wait. I randomly chose. The young lady was facing the band so I tapped her on the shoulder. She turned. I was so nervous that I could not tell you what she looked like or what she wore. I barely was able to say the magic words:

"Would you like to dance," almost forgetting to add, "...with me?"

These events happened a long time ago. The years since then have been full of events both happy and sad. I married and divorced. A son was born. He is now older than I was that night. Time should have distorted my memory of what that young lady said to me, but as television's obsessive-compulsive detective, Mr. Monk, always says: "I don't think so."

She clearly said: "No," adding, "...and don't bother me again, four-eyes!"

Did she laugh at me then, or simply turn away? I don't remember. Did I cry? No. I learned a painful lesson: Embarrassment does not kill you; it just makes you wish you were dead. I stood rooted to the spot and offered a silent prayer for the Earth to open up and devour me. It didn't happen. I knew enough to get away – what if she turned around and found me still there? Perhaps I hoped that moving would erase the pain her words had caused.

Action often follows choice, and creates more of them. That night, the choice was "In which direction should I flee?" The walk back to the far end of the gym seemed infinitely long. But worse was the vision of all the guys laughing and calling me names, the most kind, probably, was "pathetic!" Self-absorbed, I knew that everyone had seen me ask, get rejected, and be humiliated. Teenage boys can be equally cruel as girls. My retreat to the rear was thus held up by my heart's terrified pounding. Rooted in fear, only my eyes were able to move, turning to the side wall, close and safe. Unfortunately, all the floor mats were there. They were gathered up into giant orange rolls, and made the amount of space available to stand apart from the crowd dauntingly small. I then looked to the other side, but could not see it because of the crowd of girls.

If you can't go forward (onto the band-stand), to either side, or back – what do you do? Perhaps the answer was whispered into my ear by my guardian angel – I was born on the feast day of Saint Michael, the

Archangel. It may be that I came up with the thought myself, unlikely though that may be. No matter where it came from, the idea was preposterous – but there it was.

Ask another girl to dance.

*   *   *   *   *

Twenty years had passed filled with life and, luckily, interesting work. Then a routine eye-doctor visit changed things. He found a serious problem. Years of city-grit under my contact lenses had scarred both my corneas. Thankfully, the cure was straightforward: Going back to wearing my glasses for six months without putting my contacts in. It was strange wearing glasses to the office on that first day. Because of the optical characteristics of contact lenses, you actually get a wider, clearer look at the world. Glasses are more visually restrictive, not to mention the feel of their weight on your nose. But, what remained the same was the pleasure of lunch in the city with friends. I do love to eat.

Afterwards, well stuffed and very relaxed, I returned to work. Our building had been built in the 1920's and was a marvel of the Art-Deco style. This three-quarters-of-a-century-old fashion was seen everywhere, from the pinnacle of the 66-story sky-scraper, to its lobby. From the moment you entered, you were in a past era. Even the elevator doors reflected this. As I waited to go up, I was joined by a stranger. We stood in silence until the elevator's chime sounded. The doors opened and a beautiful woman stepped out. It is hard to describe when a woman's clothing leaves class behind to become risqué, but in the spirit of the "know it when you see it" camp… we looked, saw, and silently thanked our lucky stars.

We entered the elevator, the doors closed, and we began our ascent, each thinking of her enticements. The stranger then spoke:

"She'd never be interested in you because of your coke-bottles."

I was shocked by his words, feeling as if I'd been slapped. Who was he to say that? Was I wearing a sign that said "kick me!"? Didn't he know those casually spoken words would embarrass me? Was that his intention? I found myself suddenly returned to a time when my being a four-eyes mattered to me. That I was now a married, successful manager was no protection from the insecurities that suddenly surfaced from underneath a lifetime's achievements. My thoughts were in chaos.

Yet, the passage of years had done more than just give me a few grey hairs. My father's good genes and a lifetime's exercises had given me physical strength. I was now also aware of an important rule: "Never hit someone in anger, but if a sufficiently good reason exists, put them in the hospital." I pondered whether there was sufficient cause to hurt him in return; while looking at his Adam's Apple and wondering what would happen if I hit him as hard as possible, just there, with serious intent to harm. Would his head literally rip off? It was not a pleasant trip for me, in silence except for the elevator music, aware of my anger and the stupidity of my thought, but unable to shake it off.

It could have been the Archangel Michael who again intervened and rang the chime to announce the floor's arrival. Perhaps it was just dumb luck, but the doors opened, and he left. Doing so may have saved us both, but I doubt it, or at least I hope so. Even to this day, I would like to believe that I would have again chosen to dance.

*   *   *   *   *

My lesson for you here is that there are always choices – you just have to find them. My little story is meant to remind you of that. I never learned either of their names, and seriously doubt that either of my two main characters remembers me, but that does not matter.   These two moments of my life were transformative for me. In Xaverian High School's gym, in 1968, I was given one of my greatest life's lessons. In the elevator of 70 Pine Street, the lesson was reinforced, if only in glimpsing how quickly everything could be lost by forgetting the lesson:

Think about what your choices are, then choose wisely!

You can go forward, backward, or stand still; up or down; left or right. You may make a small change, or a giant one – or none at all. Tomorrow or next year – but not yesterday – are acceptable choices too. You can choose to speak, be silent, or to communicate your message in writing, by messenger, or not at all. There is always the question of which word to use. The list of choices is endless.

There are, of course, many philosophies on life: that ours is a life of pain to be endured in the spirit of purifying ourselves for the next; that we must all share each according to ability, each according to need; or simply that if I take what is yours I have more. But there is yet another way of looking at the subject.

Humankind has always strived to improve its lot and to produce things of value. Humanity has never found the status quo to be acceptable. Perhaps there is a fundamental driving force wired into us – a desire to make tomorrow better than today. It does seem that it is more satisfying to create than to destroy. Perhaps this optimistic attitude is related to hope, akin to that felt by a blind squirrel who hopes it will, and sometimes does, find a nut.

This element of hope reflects a deep personal belief: that the world will be better, and that the choices you make will help make it so. To be even more personal, I believe that you can be better, and can be so by more than just hope. You can do better than a blind squirrel. You can choose to be guided by intelligence, both yours and that of others. This will both increase the number of choices you have, and amplify the power of these choices, magnifying their outcomes. I hope that these will be spectacular for you.

Adults can never act stupidly from unexpected emotion or circumstance – but they often do. Maturity is found in knowing that the best course is to choose to dance.

I hope that you can remember this. Perhaps, even, your first steps will be to decide to read the next chapter.

Chapter 2 – WHERE IS VENUS?

Right now, wherever you are, whatever the time, point in the general direction of the planet Venus. Please, do so right now; point toward Venus.

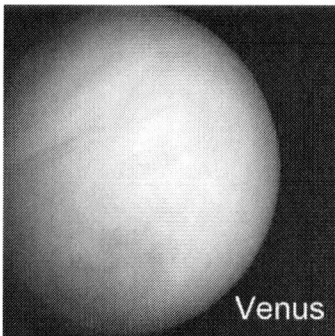

Venus

....waiting....

What do you mean this is impossible? You think that you can't?

You can. Right now, right here, correctly and you can do it with just what you know now.

Don't believe me?

Let me change tack for a moment. This book is based on the belief that you are capable of doing so much more than you might believe of yourself. This idea is not based on thinking that you will be helped by magical forces, nor that you must act strictly by yourself. One important insight for you, here, is that you have help available.

Sir Isaac Newton – the man who discovered gravity; the guy who was inspired when he saw an apple fall; who invented *The Calculus* so that he could express his ideas mathematically – said:

"If I see farther, it is only because I stand on the shoulders of giants."

These giants are those who lived before him and upon whose ideas he built. Perhaps he meant people like Johannes Gutenberg, the inventor of mechanically printed books. Isaac may have meant his teachers, without whom he would have lacked the intellectual tools he so brilliantly used. Or he could have been honoring his parents, without whom he would not have been, and who more importantly, were the two early forces in his life who taught, shaped, and guided him.

You should be reminded of Isaac Newton each time you go to the store and get change from a cash purchase or use a coin-operated vending machine. Sir Isaac served as the Chancellor of the Exchequer for England. At that time, coins were made of precious metals including silver and gold. Shopkeepers had developed the cute little habit of nipping off a bit from the coins that passed through their tills.   Coins, therefore, tended to *shrink*. He ordered the edges of all coins be *milled*, that is marked with grooves. This marking made the *nipping* practice obvious, and so ended it.   Look at the dimes and quarters in your pocket – those marks are daily proof that Sir Isaac Newton walked the Earth.

The marks of those who have preceded us are everywhere. They are many. It is impossible to list them all. Even a summary of them would make for a long read. These people, and a multitude of others, have left their impressions in and on you without your being consciously aware of it. Because of this, you have capabilities that far exceed whatever you believe possible. This chapter is about the previous sentence: to believe in your intellectual capacity.

I distinctly remember seeing the planet Venus for the first time.   Prior to that moment I believed, as you probably do, that while there are some people (besides astronomers) who know where the planets are, I was not one of them.

The journey of discovery began, by accident, in the local library. There was a poster on the wall advertising a local astronomy club's open house. It was held, weather permitting, on the third Friday of every month. Never having been to an observatory, indeed not even knowing that there was one nearby, this seemed to be an interesting way to spend an evening.

On the appointed day, my then 12-year-old son and I took a drive to see the stars. The directions took us up a lonely lane as it curved around a desolate hill. The area looked as imagined in a gothic novel: leafless branches

swaying and stray papers tumbling across the road. There even was a cemetery below, in the distance. Atop the hill, the wind was moaning as we parked the car and walked to a windowless, domed building. We opened a non-descript door and entered a large, round room dominated by the telescope in its center. The ceiling was made out of segments of sheet-metal. One of them was part of a door-assembly which had been slid open to show the sky above. Sunlight was entering the dome through the opening though it was not aligned exactly toward the setting sun.

The telescope looked to be a ten-foot long pipe mounted on a large tripod. It had some large gears below. An eyepiece above was connected by a small pipe at right angles. This eyepiece was not at its end as we expected. We were told that the main lens was eighteen inches wide. It was now pointed toward the sheet-metal ceiling. This entire setup seemed primitive, far from being as impressive as pictures of the 200-inch reflector telescope at Mt. Palomar show it to be.

Two men were puttering around, members of the amateur astronomy club. We were the only visitors. To the west, the sun slowly set, blood-red, promising a change in the weather for the better.

"Welcome." One of the men said. "Have you ever been to an observatory?"

"No," we replied. "We were very surprised to learn you were so close to our home."

He told us that he had to position both the roof and telescope. The dome rested on many automobile tires, and he used an electric motor to turn it until the opening was completely aligned toward the West. He then rotated the telescope. It too, was built to rotate driven by a series of gears, the largest ones meshing with the smallest – powered directly by another motor – turning until the telescope centered in the roof's opening. All this took less than five minutes and we were then directed to look into the eyepiece.

"You first," motioning to my son.

He climbed up onto the metal platform, grasping the rails on both sides of the steps. He had to adjust himself to be able to look into the eyepiece. There was a moment of silence as he contemplated what he was seeing, then:

"Oh, wow! This is so cool!"

His exclamation was a surprise to me. What was he seeing? Even if you magnify a star, it would seem obvious that you will only see a larger, glowing light. We had not yet been told about all the types of celestial objects that you could see from that telescope on a clear evening – the Messier objects: the double stars, the nebulae, and all the other marvelous sights in the heavens.

When he finally finished, it was my turn. I climbed up and could now see that the Sun had gone beneath the horizon leaving behind a single, bright star directly in line with the telescope. Irritatingly, my eye-glasses did not fit well against the viewer's molded eye-piece. I had to press the lens of my good eye against it hard and uncomfortably. Moving slowly, I grasped the handles provided for stability and gazed into the sky.

I did not see the bright light of a magnified star as I expected. Instead, there was an image which will stay with me all my life: a sharply-defined, black circle floating in a dark sky. The black orb was edged by a crescent of light so bright that it hurt my eye. Instead of a star, I saw a planet and knew instantly which it was. I was looking upon the planet named after the goddess of love, Venus. The knowledge, absent seconds before but clear now, made me feel instantly foolish.

Can you point in the general direction of my *discovery* now? I'll give you a hint.

There are nine planets. The name of the most distant is Pluto. Even if some have decided that Pluto is no longer a planet, it remains the name of a famous Walt Disney animated dog. You may also have heard that the tenth, planet X, has either been found, or is being sought, or is the title of a movie that you never saw. You can probably name most of the planets, right? Though you may, like most, get the order of the planets mixed up, certainly you know the first four: Mercury, Venus, Earth, and Mars.

Now do you know where Venus is at this instant?

Because Venus is the second planet from the Sun, it usually lies between us and our star, so it is normally very hard, if not impossible, to see – except under special conditions. When the sun is just below the horizon and Venus' orbit places it above the horizon it shines for all to see. This happens only in the mornings and

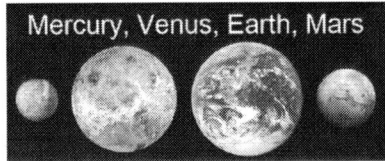
Mercury, Venus, Earth, Mars

evenings for a short period each year. This is the cause of two of Venus' other names: The Morning Star and the Evening Star.

During the day, Venus can't be seen except by very special equipment because the Sun is too bright. Looking at it would mean staring directly at the Sun. This is true, too, when the planet is on the opposite side of the Sun. It can't be seen then either. At night the Earth itself blocks our line of sight.

But you can always point in its general direction – toward the Sun. Sometimes it is a little to the right of the Sun, other times a little to the left...

...but it is always in the general direction of the Sun!

You must admit that the answer is surprisingly simple now that you have seen how the answer was generated. You must also agree that there was little in that process that you did not already know. You could have put the pieces of the puzzle together by yourself! This chapter's quiz, "Where is Venus?" might easily be about any number of subjects that you, yourself, are capable of answering in the same manner.

This is not to imply that you know the answer to everything. However, you, right now, are capable of answering far more than you thought possible; you are smarter than, and more capable than you might have believed. This is because you "stand on the shoulders of giants" both the world's greats, and your own.

And what of those questions that you cannot answer? Go find some giants. Look in the library; ask friends, teachers, or your spouse. Get on the Internet and if you don't know how, *learn!* At worst, you will improve yourself just for the effort. You might even find out that this leads you to a solution: Being able to roughly point to the right direction matters to everyone in their lives. Consider that even great baseball players *do not* get a hit 70% of the time. You can improve *your batting average* by learning to study a problem. Bring all that is within you to bear and add to your knowledge with that from giants.

Let me offer you one last thought. This is something we have experienced, surprisingly, rather often. Working to solve a problem can lead you to solving problems other than the one you started to address. You can consider why this is so.

Chapter 3 – THEY WERE, ONCE

"The moving finger writes, then having writ, moves on."

A thousand years ago, the Persian poet, Omar Khayyam, made the point that what happened in the past cannot be changed. This is not the same, however, as saying that the future is set in stone today. The idea behind this book is simple: You can improve. Tomorrow you will do what today you cannot. You will get better in a hundred ways, including: adding and refining skills, expanding your sources of information, and even dropping bad habits (but boy, this last is hard to do!).

Everyone starts out in the same way: the mystery, beauty, and even the messiness of birth. Those who survive, begin to grow, learn and move forward. All will gain experience through the passing of time in the form of new knowledge: from formal and informal education, and even from having failed at something. This is true especially for those historic figures remembered for having done great things, often in the face of long odds. Their early lives sometimes give little indication of what the future would hold for them.

This is illustrated here from a few, brief biographies. Try and solve the mystery of who they turned out to be; but even more importantly, consider whether their example applies to you. Will you do tomorrow what you have not yet done?

Germaine Greer, the Australian writer and feminist, once noted: "Human beings have an inalienable right to invent themselves..." Who will you become?

Who Are They?

His father wanted him to be an electrical engineer, but he failed the school's entrance examination. He thus found the door to his expected career was shut firmly – with him on the wrong side. A lesser institution accepted him but his four-year record there can only be described as unexceptional. In an essay that he penned there – for which he got half-marks – he described himself and his plans for the future. One line summarized it all:

"I imagine myself becoming a teacher... [due to] my lack of imagination and practical ability."

His job-hunt began after graduation. He asked many schools if they had an opening for a newly-minted teacher. Some of them held out some hope, but nothing further came from any of them. His friends were hired as teachers – but not him. He clearly did not impress anyone.

It took a year and a half for him to get work. A Technical High School brought him in to teach mathematics part-time. Needing more money than he earned there, he accepted help from a friend whose father had government connections. These were able to open the door to another job – a temporary one – but it did come with a title. He was now a *Technical Expert, Third Class*. It took two years for the government to make the position permanent and another two years for them to promote him all the way up to being *Second Class*.

Perhaps he was not recognized because he was often lost in dreams, thinking about nothing – or very little, as the case may be. Much of the work from which we now know him was done in his head. It is not cruel to say that his physical presence was not imposing. He was certainly not photogenic and was slight of build. The most famous picture of him was taken with his tongue sticking out. In every photograph you can see how he is distinguished by his hair – an unruly mop at best.

It was in those years when he worked in the government's patent office that Albert Einstein did some of his best work. His unwavering belief in the ultimate order of the Universe is illustrated by his famous quote, "God does not play dice with the Universe." Yet his revolutionary theories took the previous ideas of order and tossed them into history's wastebasket. In Einstein's world, time is affected by the speed at which you travel; light is bent by gravity; indeed, the very Universe itself is curved.

Albert Einstein

Most of Einstein's ideas have been proven true; his theories are now facts. One famous experiment occurred in 1919, only weeks before the Treaty of Versailles was signed. This treaty both ended the First World War and marked the end of Europe as it had existed. Entire empires were erased off the world map. The experiment, however, both ended the Universe as it was then known and created an entirely new one!

This experiment was simple.   Scientists carefully observed a distant star during a full eclipse of our Sun. If Einstein was right, the star would appear in a location slightly different from where it actually was. This could only happen if the starlight was bent by the gravity of the Sun.   They looked, and they saw.   This confirmed Einstein's theory.   Some deem this date to be the beginning of our modern age, a universe based on Einsteinian physics.   Perhaps, however, the real date should be marked by the day on which he failed his college entrance examination.

*   *   *   *   *

His family was a very patriotic one living in New Jersey. This angered their neighbors (it was at the time of the American Revolution). As ardent supporters of the King, they were forced to move to Canada when the English lost. During the War of 1812, a later generation of his family would continue to fight against the United States. "Al's" parents would ignore their family's history when they needed to find sanctuary from political upheaval. They returned before he was born.

He was the last of their seven children, half of whom died before adulthood. He tended to be sickly. This might account for his being a poor student. His entire formal education lasted three months. School ended when his teacher called him *addled* – a polite way of saying he was not so bright. This remark so angered his mother that she removed him from the classroom. He never went back. Mama taught him at home until he was twelve. Then he went to work selling newspapers on a railroad.

He lost almost all his hearing. Various stories try to explain why. One ascribed it to the after-effects of Scarlett Fever while another to having his ears boxed as punishment for causing a fire. The most colorful explanation described being picked up by his ears. Whatever the truth of his disability, it was one of his strengths, leading directly to his immense power of concentration. He simply did not hear distractions.

When he was fifteen he learned telegraphy spending five years working in many different cities' offices. His first patent was awarded in Boston for a device to electrically count votes. Not surprisingly to any cynic, his device was not wanted by any politician. He moved to New York vowing to never waste time inventing something that was not wanted.

His life was a continuing series of failures. His habit of working long hours affected his relationship with his first wife. Upon her death, he remarried and began a second family. Both sets of children would grow to be distant from him. He spent a decade mining iron. He was absorbed in every aspect of the firm's operations, pouring his money and energy into trying to make it a success. More time was spent in a company he formed to manufacture Portland cement. His restless mind constantly searched for innovative uses of that product. An inventor till his death, many of his developments would ultimately lose in the market to better products.

Even with his unsurpassed record of *failure*, Thomas Alva Edison's inventions transformed the world. These include the phonograph and motion pictures. All told, he has 1,093 patents granted under his name. He is perhaps best known as the father of the electric light bulb, but this might be considered another failure. He did not invent it; what he did, instead, was to take a 50-year-old idea and make it practical. This came after thousands of failures as he searched for a material to use as a filament. It was Edison, however, who invented the system by which electricity could power an entire city, and he who gave the world the ability to transform night into day at the flick of a switch.

If the measure of a man is his circle of friends, consider some of his: Henry Ford, Harvey Firestone, and Alexander Graham Bell. Yet Edison's greatest achievement was not an invention at all. The wizard of Menlo Park was so named because he built the first modern research laboratory in that New Jersey town – a *machine* to invent inventions.

*   *   *   *   *

Her friends and family called her by a nickname, "Manya," but formally, she was Maria Sklodowska. She was born in Warsaw, then a provincial city of the Czar's Empire. Poland had ceased to exist over 50 years before her birth, but her parents were determined to preserve Polish culture at all cost. She thus was raised to be Polish. This patriotism carried a high price: They suffered financially, it cost them their health, and even their lives.

Manya was denied admission to Warsaw's University because of her sex – women were denied the opportunities that education provides. They were simply not allowed in. She and her sister did not accept this (are you surprised) and attended a clandestine *floating school*. It met at night and changed locations frequently to avoid detection by the Czar's police. Manya would put her dreams of getting a formal education on hold while her older sister went abroad to study. To help pay for her sister's medical studies in Paris, Manya took a job as a tutor of a factory owner's children. She did so for five years, saving her pennies to be able to follow her sister abroad. Leaving her family and native land was difficult and costly – she lost her very name. In Paris she became *Marie*.

Money was scarce and she was ill prepared for her studies at the Sorbonne but hard work prevailed. Often she would be so consumed by her efforts that she would forget to eat. She would not only graduate but would become the first woman to receive a doctorate in France. The committee of examiners declared that her work had done more for science than any previous thesis.

She would meet, love, and marry a man ten years her elder. When she needed a laboratory to pursue her studies, it would first be in the crowded and damp storeroom of the municipal school where her husband, Pierre, was a professor. Later she would move into an abandoned shed nearby. They would continue working together until his death. Sadly, this happened too soon. He was crushed by a heavily laden horse cart. Afterwards, she just kept on working, until the day of her own death by a work-related disease.

Her patriotism is remembered by all chemists and physicists who, in learning the Periodic Table of the

Elements encounter number sixty-six – *Polonium* – which she named after her native land. This remarkable woman received a Nobel Prize in Physics – the first ever won by a woman. She then was awarded second in Chemistry. She was the first person to win the Nobel Prize twice. Her family, even more remarkably, owns another. The third Prize was awarded to her daughter in recognition of her years working with Manya. Today *mama* is remembered by her married name, Madame Curie, and her gift to the world was the science of radioactivity.

*   *   *   *   *

He was born just days after the troops of General Robert E. Lee's Army of Virginia marched to, fought at, and retreated from the gentle hills of Gettysburg in the climactic battle of America's Civil War. The family farm was 450 miles from that bloodbath. Its name would become synonymous with another great battle: that which ended the agrarian world with its slow rhythms and horse-drawn wagons. The oldest of six children born into a prosperous farming family, he was seemingly destined to inherit that life. The river his family had used for the farm's water was always important to him. There he rose to fame.

His education began in a one-room schoolhouse. Apprenticed at the age of sixteen, he spent three years learning the skills of a machinist. He returned to the family farm where he occasionally and reluctantly assisted with farm chores, but most often his hands were black with oil as he repaired steam engines or overhauled the farm's machinery.

He would later recount that the greatest day of his life was when he married Clara. This almost did not happen. Her mother thought that, at twenty, she was too young. Mama made the eager couple wait two years. After the wedding, he went to work operating a sawmill to support his new family. His familiarity with steam engines would lead him into an industry that had just been born. He became an engineer in one of Thomas Edison's new power-generating plants. Perhaps the great man's inventiveness rubbed off, for he too became motivated to invent. His first attempt at building a product was the *Quadricycle*. This was a 4-wheeled buggy steered with a boat-like tiller – though the idea was not his alone.

He failed twice in starting companies to build and sell his products. It took seven years after his invention first took shape that the company which would bear his name was incorporated. Five years would pass until the product destined to make him world-famous was

introduced. Ten years more, its sales would account for half of the market. This demand led him to build the River Rouge Plant, the world's largest industrial complex, on land near the family farm on the banks of the River of the same name. This facility would employ 81,000 and its buildings would provide some seven million square feet of floor space. Over 15,000,000 of his Model 'T' cars were manufactured there. They were available "in any color you want, as long as it's black."

Dearborn, Michigan would lose its peace and quiet to the industry he helped create. Nearby Detroit would become world-renown as the center of automobile manufacturing. Henry Ford might still be smiling as the innovations he fostered, including the assembly line, have kept *Ford* operating for over one-hundred years. His family is still at the tiller, guiding it – beginning with his only son, whose name you might also know – Edsel.

*   *   *   *   *

You know her name. You have probably seen one of the many movies that they made about her and might even be able to name one of the actresses who won Oscars for their performance in them. But her fame masks many contradictions. Though she became world-famous, you probably cannot recall a single of the dozen books she authored. She was a world-traveler who met kings and a dozen U.S. presidents, but was never able to travel by herself. There are city streets named in her honor around the world, including in Spain and Israel, but she never learned to drive. Sadly, though she was a voice for many who were helpless, she also seemed to inspire an enormous number of cruel jokes at her expense.

She was born to a Southern family during the Reconstruction Period after the American Civil War. As a toddler, she contracted a serious disease that left her severely handicapped. She remained a virtual invalid until the age of seven when her parents hired a live-in teacher. It took a month to learn to spell her first word, but she would eventually be admitted to, and graduate from, Harvard University's woman's branch, Radcliff. She became the first deaf and blind person to earn a Bachelor of Arts degree.   Eventually she would learn to read English, French, German, Greek and Latin.

People around the world would flock to meet Helen Keller and to listen to her speak. This she did forcefully as an advocate of women's suffrage, workers' rights, and against war itself. Considered a political extremist, her socialist views were glossed over in the press so that the public was not aware of them – though she desperately wanted otherwise. Of all that she did, the least was the introduction of the Akita breed of dog to the United States.

She was honored in life by many nations, including her own which awarded her the Presidential Medal of Freedom. Honors continued after her death. Her face now adorns on the quarter of her native Alabama and a statue of her is in the U.S. Capitol. It is inscribed in both English and Braille:

"The best and most beautiful things in the world cannot be seen or even touched; they must be felt with the heart."

She was laid to rest after a service held at the National Cathedral in Washington, DC. There her ashes rest, next to those of her constant companions: Anne Sullivan and Polly Thompson.

*   *   *   *   *

Growing up in a working-class neighborhood in England and attending a parochial school, she was always thinking of fanciful stories to tell her younger sister. Known simply as "Jo," she was a bookish, clever girl but didn't seem to have many ambitions – except to be a writer. But none of her scribbles ever managed to gain any attention.

Reluctantly obeying her mother's wishes, she studied French in college. After graduation, she took several jobs in London until she became a bi-lingual secretary for *Amnesty International*. She enjoyed working for this charity but, on her own time, she was still fixated on her chosen avocation – writing. Slowly, an idea for a storyline and a unique set of characters congealed in her mind and she began outlining a fantastical, whimsical fantasy world.

It was at this time that her mother, to whom she was very close, passed away. This event seems to have caused her to be even less interested in her job and more determined to work on her book. However, one must eat; she moved to Portugal to teach English.

She married and had a daughter but the marriage didn't last. She returned to Britain as a single parent considering herself "the biggest failure I knew." She suffered from depression and even contemplated suicide. She was forced into taking public assistance but found a stable job which changed her outlook. But more importantly to her, she was able to finish her book – typing it on an old manual typewriter.

Many publishers rejected her queries for over a year. Finally, she located a small publishing house willing to take a chance because the publisher's eight-year-old daughter had given an enthusiastic recommendation to the yet-to-be-edited manuscript. The publisher gave her a small advance but cautioned her to keep her day job. Much to everyone's amazement, within a few weeks, sales of the book skyrocketed and the public began clamoring for additional volumes. Jo was only too happy to oblige as she could now spend all of her time writing.

Seven *Harry Potter* books and movies have made J. K. Rowling one of the richest women in the world – and a large contributor to *Amnesty International*. The lush, vivid, ingenious world she created has been credited with increasing children's desire to read at a time when computers seem to monopolize their attention. Her fantasy series will certainly continue to be beloved by children of all ages.

*   *   *   *   *

You were born of the union of your parents and entered the world much smaller than you are today. Language came several years later. Reading and writing came years later. You have thus a history of continuing to improve yourself, even if you didn't know that you were doing so. While it is true that some are lucky, usually the rule is:

"The harder you work, the luckier you get!"

Each of the men and women in this chapter began as you did. That you know them – that history remembers them – comes from years of their learning and hard work.

Their education might not have been formal, but it was there nonetheless. Each of them grew as they battled through life. Success they may have had, but failure too.

No matter where you are now, what you are doing, or even the plans you have, tomorrow is yet to be written. Improving yourself will only help make your story come out better. Doing so takes effort, but it can also be fun. But for you, as for all those who you have just read about:

The story's end is not always dictated by its beginning...

it can be improved...

and so can you!

Read to advance your purposes, but remember that things do not just happen, you have to make them happen for you! Reading is critical, but that does not mean you cannot improve its utility by what your choices are, by how often you indulge, and by how you read.

One last thing: You will enjoy reading and you will pass on its love to those you love – this is a hope, pleasure, and obligation.

~SKILLS SECTION~

Chapter 4 – SPEAK BETTER

Learning to talk is not hard and this is not a surprise as you have seen babies go from sounds, through words and into language (even if you don't remember doing this). Tots begin this process when they are very young – possibly when they are in the womb. Amazingly, they do so without caring which language they are imbibing of the literally thousands of languages, including English, Russian, Urdu, and Mandarin.

| Speak better | Говори лучше | بات بہتر | 说得更好 |

Over the years, talking becomes so natural that it is virtually impossible to imagine ever not having been able to do so. As we develop, our ability to talk improves to the point where we can do it at any time, without fear. True, some have impediments – stuttering for one – but for the vast majority of us, the question is not whether or how to speak, but when to shut up after opening our mouths.

Speaking is different from *talking*, and is also high on the list of personal fears. The *Book of Lists* places the fear of speaking in front of a group as the #1 fear; the next is the fear of heights. The #7 fear is of dying, followed by flying, then of loneliness. Some 40% of the adult population admits that public speaking is their greatest fear.

You can lessen that fear and improve your ability to speak in public. This is not as hard as you may think, simply because you probably have never been taught how to do so. This lesson is less about overcoming the fear than it is about self-improvement. Being better at public speaking (even when the public is a small group in your living room) is ever so important. There are a wide variety of personal and professional benefits, but you already know that.

The Rules

Rule #1: Never under any circumstance, never, ever speak to a group in public.

Please re-read the first rule. Now do so again, and if you can, say it aloud. Learning and thoroughly understanding the first speaking rule will help you significantly. The rule has been written in such a way as to make it stick in your mind – if only that you cannot help but question it. Now, here is Rule #1 again, slightly reworded:

Only talk to individuals – even when together as a group – *one at a time*!

Barack Obama at Democratic National Convention, Denver, 2008

It is easy to know to whom you are talking; it is the person you have made eye contact with. Look into their eyes and try to see their soul; he/she may be looking for yours. Doing so can transform what otherwise might be an awkward situation into a warm and intimate one. Talking to one person is what you have done all your life – but even this can be improved with practice. Consider how many people you meet who talk to your belly button or to the air over your head. Are you one of them? In a one-on-one conversation, why are those people who look you in the eyes so memorable? The answer is simple: They are few. The rest have either never been told to do so, or have forgotten to do so.

Make all speeches into *one-on-one*, warm conversations.

The first rule is the key to simplifying and improving your ability to perform (which is why it is called the *act* of public speaking). This assumes that you actually have something that you want to – or must – say.

If you having nothing to say, *keep your mouth shut*. Even this most mundane of actions – keeping silent – attests to your competence. Too many open their mouths and insert their foot. Don't be one of them.

The American financier, Bernard Baruch, once said that the presentation of an idea almost counts for more than the idea itself. There is a great deal of truth in that comment!

Rule #2: Know the one thing that needs saying!

Can't help you to determine what needs to be said, but instead offer the following:

- ✓ People are drowning under information. Don't add to the deluge; get to the point and be clear.

✓ "...sorry, what did you say?" People have short attention spans and forget quickly. Tell your audience what to expect; when you plan to talk about three things, say that to start, and be memorable.

✓ Information should be condensed. Prioritize and be concise.

✓ Things stick better when they are presented in various ways: text, lists, images, audio/video, graphs, comparisons, etc.

✓ Deliver value. It is not all about you. Engage the audience. Only then can you do what you intend, whether to inform, persuade, motivate, or entertain – remember that these are all different and bring costs to the listener.

Rule #3: Prepare!

Time is a precious gift and, if you have it available to you, use it well and prepare. This is what professional speakers – including the great ones – do, even if you don't see it. Preparation makes your speaking better, indeed, much better. Preparation should not be seen by your audience but they will recognize its results.

Your success on any occasion is heavily influenced by how well you prepare. You can construct your speech, objection, presentation, etc. and make it better by whatever measure you need: briefer, sharper, more visual, stronger, funnier, etc. Try multiple alternatives and do not hesitate to discard what does not work. Strengthen what is weak. Preparation can be low-tech, done anywhere, and at any time (beforehand). Use sticky-notes; write things out (never forget that paper is cheap); ask your friends or co-workers for input on whether you are clear – or persuasive. Preparation can be hard work, but the reward you get for doing so is enormous.

There are several things to consider:

✓ *The objective:* What are you trying to do: inform, persuade, motivate, or entertain? For each, what needs saying will differ – as will how it is said.

✓ *The audience:* Are they friendly, skeptical, or well educated? Knowing your audience makes a difference in the way you approach each situation. They certainly need to be told about the problems or opportunities that you plan to discuss – and the benefits to the solutions you offer, particularly if these solutions affect your audience! Indeed, that may be the only thing that catches their attention. The how or the mechanism of your speech is of less interest – at least until their attention has been achieved.

✓ *What needs saying:* Is it clear and concise? Do you have a list of things – how many? Have an appropriate order and know their relationships and priorities. Anticipate questions that will come up – and have answers ready. Don't be afraid to edit what you have come up with early; don't fear deleting where appropriate. Condense multiple information points into a smaller number of categories.

✓ *How to support your ideas:* Find useful facts and use them appropriately. Develop a simple storyline. Have examples ready – both of where your ideas worked and where they didn't. Put a human face on the situation.

✓ The structure of your talk:

◇ There are many different ways to begin speaking including just spitting out the most important point. Some believe in always telling a joke, but this may be the wrong strategy depending on the circumstances. Create and consider different versions of your first sentence and paragraph. The one requirement is that your audience is clearly told what you intend to talk about.

◇ The main body of your talk expands the story. As you create it, think of it as just a few individual words; don't worry about having lots of verbiage for each – you will add that later. Use three to seven points. Put them into whatever order makes sense: time sequence, problem/solution, prioritized list – whatever. When you are satisfied, consider how each version will sound. Use examples and illustrative jokes where needed.

◇ Last, there is the close. This can take any one of a number of forms. Among them are: the "tell them the one thing you told 'em," which means to simply restate your opening idea to reinforce your point; the "ask for the order," where you politely request your audience's agreement; or the "now go out and do...," when you try to excite your audience with a call-to-action. Try various versions to find the most powerful.

◇ Allow for questions. Try to identify those which might be asked and be prepared for them.

Decide whether to answer them immediately and risk being derailed; to write them down as asked, parking them until later; or whether to have a Q/A session at the end. These alternatives may not happen, but then again, they might.

You might only get a chance to prepare while others are talking. This might only be seconds or minutes. Find the one thing you need to say. Begin your preparation by considering that there are options: big through small. Just that short pause gives you time to think about where in that range you stand. Must you take a position now? There are many other tricks you can use in these situations. These will become habits over time. Habits get born, are nourished, and grow into strong limbs upon which to stand. Start in front of a group and only talk to individuals!

Rule #4: Practice, Practice, PRACTICE!

Practice is the times you say it right before having to say it. You may have heard that you cannot practice enough but the actual numbers may be a surprise. Professionals can spend between *10 and 50 minutes* preparing and practicing *FOR EACH MINUTE THEY HAVE TO SPEAK!* That is why their product seems so good – they've worked hard at it. So should you.

Practicing begins by going over what you want to say in your head. The good news is that no one will laugh at those attempts. The bad is that there is no feedback from anyone else. Thought sessions are important and can be done anywhere. Later, practice aloud. Talk to the chair, to the dog, and to the mirror. Make a video of yourself and watch it. Try watching it with the sound on and off. You will see some of what the audience will see. Practice in front of someone and ask for criticism. During your practice sessions, anything can be revised and improved – what and how it is said or seen. Practice the changes.

The most important parts of what you are going to say are the beginning (and even more importantly, the first sentence) and the ending. Practice these. Try to see if they are effective. Is the point you want to make clear? Try other ways of expressing yourself. Write them down, and read them aloud. Are they too long, too complex, or just nonsensical? Now is the time to get it right.

The objective of all this work is not to memorize, but to improve it and learn to deliver the best speech you can. You do not want to give a meaningless verbatim recitation, but rather to be stone-solid and extremely confident. Practice helps cure flaws and provides a foundation with which to deal with any unexpected problem that will arise – and they do. Professional actors and dancers look at themselves in a mirror. You should too. Notice that no one can see inside you to your fears or insecurities. Why many will not do a trial run is a mystery. Perhaps they feel it is cheating or a waste of time. It is not. It is being smart!

Rule #5: Be the Speaker

Here is what might be considered bad news: Over half of the impact of any speech comes from the audience looking at the speaker. Through their eyes pass information that conveys your character, competence, composure, and charisma. Probably the most important element that they can see is your sincerity. An old joke emphasizes this: "If you can't be sincere, fake it." The good news is that you are replete in all these elements and can, with very little work, convey this to the audience.

It is very hard to hide a person's character. This is another reason to be confident – because you have a character. Ask your mother, if you doubt us. She'll say you are a character! Those who will make a judgment will do so, first, by what they see. Stand tall and don't fidget (you remember hearing those words once before!). Dress professionally. Your appearance is very important. Dressing and grooming well will give you the air of believability. While you shouldn't judge a book by its cover, the fact is that people do all the time. Above all, if it is appropriate to do so, smile! When you practice in the mirror, look to see if your smile is real. You can do all these things, and more.

If you are talking about yourself, your opinion, or any of a number of other topics, recognize that you are the world's leading expert on that subject. This fact should not be a surprise. Preparation (including all that time on research) gave you a solid foundation upon which to build. You are not just *winging it*, but rather have become a master of the subject.

Having at your fingertips all the needed information will build your confidence. You can go both deep and wide about the subject – to anyone (to any one)! Practice polishes your ability to convey the solid information you possess. When you do all these things, you can relax and be seen as being composed. People like those who are composed – as you will be.

Rule #6: Talk

Having created, then practiced, all that is necessary is to find someone to talk to. You are ready. Take a deep breath. Straighten your body. Make sure that your notes are where you placed them. If you need to, have some water available in case your mouth gets dry. Now smile!

Begin by talking to someone in the room who is far away – that way you can pitch your voice to them and everyone will hear you clearly. You might start with a simple, "Fred, can you hear me?" This allows you to calibrate your voice and notifies your audience that you are about to begin. If you ask a question, wait for a reply because doing so shows that you are in control. If Fred does not answer, assume he does not hear you. Try it again, louder to a different person: "Mary, how's my voice?"

Did you remember to look into their eyes? Talking to any one person is easy. Do it for less than a minute – you don't want to stare at only one person and be seen as

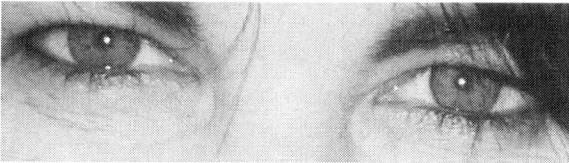

being creepy. Do talk to him or her for more than a second because you have to make a connection. Once you have engaged the person that you are talking to, move onto another person, perhaps on the other side of the room. Engaging multiple individuals over time increases the audience's sense of intimacy.

Each time you have practiced, your voice has gotten more professional. Your use of "ummm" or "like" and all the rest of the meaningless verbal tics has diminished.

Increased self-confidence allows you to avoid *up-speak* –
where every statement sounds like a question as your
inflection turns up at the end of each. Your statements
will sound authoritative because you are, after all, an
authority on the subject. Your voice has gotten clearer
and stronger. Your practices and all your developing
experience have given you the ability to vary your
loudness, pitch, and speed.

People love to hear their names, so use them. Do not
rush your words. Give the person you are talking to time
to absorb what you are saying. You've got a structure:
opening, middle, and end. Make the transitions between
sections clear but smooth. Don't confuse. Simplify. All
that preparation has helped make you appear as being
honest and interesting.

You are the only one of this particular model that was
ever made, or that will ever be made. Be proud of that
and like yourself for that. You will do fine and with
practice, even better.

Tricks

Speaking in public is most people's top fear, and so,
ways to improve your skills are presented as *tricks* so that

you do not think that only
a professional speaker can
speak well. These tricks-
of-the-trade are small
things to help improve
your overall experience.
Now, take a deep breath
and cynically use another
trick without worrying.

✓ *Be early!* This is the very simplest trick. Meet the people to whom you will be talking beforehand. Don't try to learn everyone's name, but get a few. Ask them about their expectations. Look at the room. Does it have everything you'll need (whiteboard, projector, water, whatever)? Being early gives time to move things around and make yourself more comfortable.

✓ *Use Quotes, Figures, and Images!* "Albert Einstein said…" or "The President noted…" These, selected in advance and casually used, reinforce your point. References to sources, sample data, historical facts, etc. all help support your point and make you sound like you know what you're talking about – and you do.

✓ *Use props!* Remember that you are your greatest prop! Still, a huge pile of paper illustrates the complexity of the law, a glass of sludge, a big rusty nail…

✓ *Use Humor!* Feel free not to start with a joke if that is not you. In your preparation, you can identify illustrative jokes and know where they might best be used. You don't have to say them, but you can, depending on the feel of the audience. But know your audience and avoid off-color jokes – you never know who you might be offending.

✓ *Ask a question!* This is hard, but only the first time you do it. What if there is no answer? Wait. Feel the silence. Keep relaxed. Scan the people and wait. Eventually someone will answer – and you will own all of them as you have established that when you ask, someone must answer. This power is doubly reinforced if you opened with "can you hear me?" and waited until someone answered.

✓ *Use silence!* When you are not talking to someone, be quiet. Don't feel the need to babble on. Be quiet between sections. Let the message be absorbed. Let people think. Let them wonder. Try this: "I have three things that concern me." Pause. "The first is the most important." Pause.

✓ *Use notes!* Bring index cards with an outline, key words, whatever, clearly written. When you need to look at your notes – and you will – shut up, find what you need, read it, and smile – you are amused at yourself for forgetting. We all do it. Now, look at one person and talk to him or her.

✓ *Have excess material!* You can use it if needed, but just having it will show that you are prepared.

✓ *End early!* Staying over-long is a crime; it's best to keep 'em wanting more. You always want to be respectful of your audience's time.

✓ *Do not shoot yourself in the foot!* Avoid saying "…don't know what I'm talking about" nor anything to belittle yourself. If you respect the time of the person you are talking to and focus on his / her needs you will get respect in return. Self-deprecating humor, however, is useful.

✓ *Be prepared for what will go wrong!* Things do go wrong. You may be asked a difficult or unexpected question. You will have canned answers for pre-identified questions. But for questions you didn't expect, write down the question – even on a whiteboard – it will give you time to think of an answer. If an answer is not forthcoming, offer to get back to the person later. Bring a spare marker. You may drop your marker. If you do, ignore it, use the spare, finish what you are saying and when a natural break occurs – pick it up.   If your talk involves a computer or projector, bring backup media. Your presentation should be on a CD and a thumb drive. You never know when 'Murphy' will decide to crash your laptop or blow-out the projector bulb.

✓ *Be yourself!* This is both easy and hard. You will want to be someone – anyone else. Don't be. You are only talking to one person and you are prepared. If you have forgotten their name, laugh, smile, shake your head, apologize, and ask their name. Repeat it and hit yourself on the forehead. You are human as we all are.

Stage Fright

Since speaking in public is many people's top fear, admit your terror if it exists. It can hurt and even debilitate you. Confront it. Think about what is the worst thing that will happen. Say them aloud. Your head won't explode nor will your pants catch fire. Remember that embarrassment does not kill, it just makes you wish you were dead – and it happens to all.

There is the advice, "Imagine your audience sitting in their underwear." This is twice a mistake. First, you don't have an *audience*; you are talking to one person. Second, are you hanging out with exhibitionists or want them to be so?

Stress is physical, emotional, and mental. Do physical things to help relieve it. Push very hard against a wall, trying to give the wall all your worries. Take a deep breath. Stretch. Go for a brief walk. Go to bed early the night before. Eat well. Go to the bathroom – and not just for the obvious – look into a mirror and smile at yourself. Shake your head at how you look stressed. Laugh and smile at yourself again. Do not chew gum or suck on a mint during your speech. It might be considered rude.

Remind yourself of all your preparation. You are very ready with notes in your pocket should you need them, a clear and practiced message, with friends out there...the list is long. You will be having a conversation with only one person so you can ignore everyone else.

Most of all, you are doing this because you choose to and not for any other reason. You could be sitting in the audience, silent. They all are.

Do It in a Different Language

Learning a second language (or third) can help you in many ways. Bi-lingual speakers are in demand. But more to the point of this chapter, learning a new language will help you become a better speaker in your native tongue. The process can actually improve your grammar and vocabulary as you notice similarities and differences between the languages.

Babies do it, and you did it, so you can do so again. What you have never been told is that learning a language is relatively easy, but it takes time – think of all the hours babies and children took to acquire their level of mastery.

There is good news. You only need about one thousand words to know a language –

haltingly and very badly. Five-thousand words and you sound like an uneducated peasant. With twenty-five thousand you'll sound relatively educated.

There is better news. We all start with many words in virtually any language already in our heads. *Ma* is virtually universal. *Telephone*, or some variant, is too as are many other modern or technical words: *Google*, *iPod*, *System*. You probably know the numbers in Spanish or in German already. They are similar in Romanian, Portuguese, Italian, and in many other languages. Numbers are useful in many ways: in Mandarin the days of the week are *number+day*.

The question is how to be like a child and get the time. Consider that even as a baby is playing with her feet, she is listening. Set the radio in your car to a foreign station and leave it there. Wear headphones and play a book-on-tape. Listen to it over and over. Every now and then look up what a word means – you'll be surprised how often a single word's meaning clarifies many around it! Watch closed-captioned soap operas. Get your news from foreign websites or newspapers (will they be around in the future?). The news is usually written to a simpler standard – 8th grade level for most papers. You could even take a language course.

Don't forget to practice. Talk with native speakers. You'll be pleased by their reaction. Language is a window to a different culture. So much gets revealed that is otherwise hidden.

Conclusion

Our verbal chapter did not cover every single thing you need. No single book can do that. Experts have lists of tricks that seem to go on forever and they are constantly expanding and refining them.

Our main point in this chapter is very simple. Though you have never been taught to speak, you can talk – to one person. Everything else can be added. Over time, with energy, you can get a lot better! It will even get to be kind of fun.

Chapter 5 – READ BETTER

Thank you for reading these words; twice if reading them in a purchased copy of this book.

Teachers have always assigned us books to read. It is sad to admit, but for many of us, rarely did we enjoy the works we were forced to laboriously absorb. Those teachers' intentions were good. It's just that the purpose of their assignments may not have been made clear enough.

Let us begin by reminding you: "In the land of the blind, the one-eyed man is king."

Sometimes just knowing a little more than someone else is enough. You can win, over those who know less, with surprisingly little additional information. This is certainly true in playing cards, where winning can depend on knowing what seems like almost insignificantly small details: the number of picture cards left in the deck, the number of spades remaining, or more obtusely, even a particular player's emotional state. To know more can be as simple as reading a particular book. The question, then, is why would anyone not read?

There are many possible reasons to be reluctant to read. Sadly, there are those who suffer from any of a number of syndromes which make reading difficult. Then, there are those who have not learned to read –

some who are gifted athletically and have always been pushed through their classes to support their sports' careers.

Most people probably find reading too inefficient; they are used to instant gratification where long periods of concentration are not required. Unfortunately, our society has caused this condition. There are many sources of information that are more *instant* than reading a book (television, radio, many web sites, etc.). But the fact is that reading can be more edifying, more thorough, and more satisfying.

Reading doesn't necessarily require a book. There are reams of valuable and authoritative information available in magazines and on certain web sites like Wikipedia.org. Avail yourself of their bounty. If you find that you have been unable or unwilling to commit the time and concentration needed to read a book, consider your priorities. Try reading a good one, you may find that the time spent is more valuable to you than what you have been doing – even if that value is only in enjoyment.

There might even be those who feel that gleaning information from a book might be considered *cheating* or that you are a thief for having taken things out of a book. For those of this last category, get over it. The reason that anyone puts anything into a book is that they want you to benefit from the sharing of their knowledge – just don't re-publish it as your own! For those who have difficulty reading, there are many avenues available to get help – or discover *books-on-tape*.

Back to High School

In New Jersey's Seton Hall Prep, there is a painting dedicated to a high-school alumnus hanging on the wall of one of the school's corridors. This is not surprising, except to note that this one is in memory of a man who was awarded the <u>Congressional Medal of Honor</u>. He had been a soldier, but did not carry a gun. Ordained a Catholic Priest, he volunteered for duty in Vietnam and served

Congressional Medal of Honor

there as a Chaplain. He fell during an action in which his unit came under heavy fire; dying after repeatedly rescuing wounded members of the unit while ignoring his own multiple wounds. We here remember and honor Father Charles J. Watters.

I saw his portrait while walking down that same school corridor, and was moved to examine the many other things on its walls. One of them was a list of the students who had received the *National Merit Scholar* award in the last year. The number was impressive, but it had had dropped by half over time. There was nothing to indicate why this was true but it did prompt the question, "What could be done to raise the performance of the students?" or more succinctly, "How can kids be made smarter?"

One answer was to get them to read more. Reaching out to some friends who headed the English Departments in a number of schools, they stressed a decline in the number of books read by the students. The reasons given were many: television, electronic games, and the huge number of amusements available via the Internet. They cited specific examples, like the once successful – now virtually abandoned – summer-book programs that had been fine-tuned over many years. Professional educators at all levels agree that reading is critical to improving a student's performance and is invaluable for anyone wishing to improve their intellectual abilities. Besides ingesting information, the act of reading improves grammar, increases vocabulary, enhances your ability to concentrate and focus, and widens your perspective on the world.

So how do you get your children to read? How about you?

Too Much Information

No matter what you call it: data, information, knowledge, teachings – there is virtually an infinite amount of it out there. That may seem intimidating, but it does not excuse you from trying to know more. Consider it to be a challenge, or a motivation, as in: those who die with the most, win. Walter Wriston, the fabled chairman of Citibank, had a very specific take on it, saying: "Information about money has become almost as important as money itself." This chapter is more general about advocating the gathering of information, offering that there are choices of what to read, whether for fun or need. Both reasons for reading are legitimate and should be pursued continually. Make it a hobby and spend time each day reading.

You are faced with many choices of what to read. Choose wisely but not obsessively. There is a lifetime to peruse the very many short stories, poems, essays, reports, articles, and novels on the ever-expanding menu. Many new choices are being made available electronically to you including physical works never available before; information in never-before-existing databases; and new forms of writing, e.g. blogs.

What to Read

There is help in choosing from the oceans of written information available. There are lists: of the world's greatest books, of the Pulitzer Prize winners, of best sellers, of the most influential books, etc. You might also ask those who you respect what they read and would like to recommend.

Here is a short compendium, broken down by subject that might be of use. This list merely indicates both the size of the ocean in which you can swim and the quality of the fish in it for you to dine upon and digest.

There are many great books on the human condition including Steinbeck: *Grapes of Wrath* and *Of Mice and Men*, Lee: *To Kill a Mockingbird*, Walker: *The Color Purple*, Faulkner: *The Sound and the Fury*, Hemingway: *The Sun Also Rises*, Miller: *Tropic of Cancer* and Hawthorne: *The Scarlet Letter*. To these you might add the very many known as Epics: Mitchell: *Gone with the Wind*, Hugo: *Les Miserables*, Tolkien: *The Lord of the Rings* and Tolstoy: *War and Peace*.

There are always the romance novels: McCullough: *The Thornbirds*, Austen: *Pride and Prejudice*, Joyce: *Lady Chatterley's Lover*, Leroux: *The Phantom of the Opera* and Pasternak: *Doctor Zhivago.* And then there are the Westerns: Schaefer: *Shane*, Wister: *The Virginian*, Clark: *The Ox-Bow Incident*, Swarthout: *The Shootist*, Grey:

Riders of the Purple Sage, and London: *Call of the Wild*. You might get into mysteries whose queen remains Agatha Christie or horror, from: Stoker: *Dracula*, Shelley: *Frankenstein*, King: *The Shining*, Blatty: *The Exorcist* and Benchley: *Jaws*.

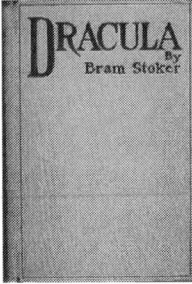

Tastes vary with some preferring science-fiction: Herbert: *Dune*, Asimov: *Foundation*, Clarke: *2001: A Space Odyssey*, Bradbury: *Martian Chronicles*, Dick: *Do Androids Dream of Electric Sheep* and Verne: *Twenty Thousand Leagues Under the Sea*. Others prefer the Crime genre: Dostoyevsky: *Crime and Punishment* and Harris: *Silence of the Lambs*. In any case, this is a very brief sample of some fiction novels, books that are for your entertainment but still manage to convey much of value.

Equally interesting – perhaps surprisingly – can be the non-fiction books. They could be about individuals – biographies: Manchester: *American Caesar* and *The Last Lion* – or about medicine like: Root-Bernstein: *Honey, Mud, Maggots and other Medical Marvels*, Freud: *The Interpretation of Dreams*, and Bliss: *The Discovery of Insulin*.

Non-fiction can be about masses of people – history: Brown: Bury My Heart at Wounded Knee, Gibbon: The History of the Decline and Fall of the Roman Empire, and Solzhenitsyn: The Gulag Archipelago – or about war: Heller: Catch-22, Shaara: The Killer Angels, Crane: The Red Badge of Courage, Ibanez: The Four Horsemen of the Apocalypse, Remarque: All Quiet of the

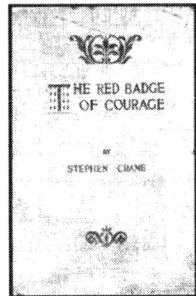

Western Front, McPherson: Battle Cry of Freedom, and Adams: Watership Down.

They might describe why things happen from any of a number of perspectives – religious: *The Bible, the Koran*, Saint Augustine: *Confessions*, Douglas: *The Robe*, Greene: *The Power and the Glory* – or philosophical: Nietzsche: *Thus Spoke Zarathustra*, and Thoreau: *Civil Disobedience* – or political: Orwell: *Nineteen Eighty-Four* and *Animal Farm*, Mill: *On Liberty*, Machiavelli: *The Prince*.

While the categories provided above were for both fiction and non-fiction, the list goes on and on. There are books on technology: Rhodes: *The Making of the Atom Bomb*, Hawking: *A Brief History of Time* or on giving advice, even from the 17th century: Gracian: *The Art of Worldly Wisdom*. There are books that moved millions' hearts and minds: Friedan: *The Feminine Mystique*, Carson: *Silent Spring* and others responsible for great evil: Hitler: *Mein Kampf*, Mao: *Quotations from Chairman Mao Tse-tung* (The Little Red Book), and Marx and Engels: *Manifesto of the Communist Party*.

There are authors whose writings have resulted in bodies of work memorable for a single character: Burroughs' Tarzan, Howard's Conan, Rowling's Harry Potter, Doyle's Sherlock Holmes, and Fleming's Bond, James Bond. Others who are equally prolific include Clancy, Grafton, Zane, Cussler, and Asimov. Read them with pleasure. Find other authors that you enjoy – and learn from them.

There are other types of written work. Consider the plays by Shakespeare: *Hamlet*, et al, or by Gibson: *The Miracle Worker*, Miller: *Death of a Salesman*, Beckett: *Waiting for Godot*, and Hansberry: *A Raisin in the Sun*.

How about a short story? Try: Jackson: *The Lottery*, Irving: *The Legend of Sleepy Hollow*, Poe: *The Telltale Heart*, and Henry: *The Gift of the Magi*. Or perhaps you prefer poetry: Whitman: *Song of Myself*, and *O Captain*, Byron: *She Walks in Beauty*, Poe: *The Raven* and Kipling: *The Seven Seas*.

You can also opt for a wide variety of magazines, both from the stands and delivered electronically to you from: *The Economist*, *Fortune*, and *Time* to *Mad Magazine* or *Playboy*. There are also essays, newspapers, journals, and online blogs, forums, wikis, and all the rest. Each choice gives you something different.

You have been urged to read, and to choose your materials wisely. It is also important to be critical of what you read. Think, analyze, and question. Do not, however, make the mistake of assuming that because you can read the words, you fully understand the message. Seek out critique – you will be surprised, that is a guaranty.

Here is one example. Herman Wouk wrote *The Caine Mutiny* – famously made into a major motion picture starring Humphrey Bogart. He plays a Captain of a small ship in the Pacific during WWII whose actions are considered cowardly by his officers and crew. He seems to be the villain of the story. Yet he is really the hero of the story. There is no other, no matter how much the reader desires to find another who qualifies.

The book addresses what happens to a man after he can no longer be a hero. The captain had fought his war in the Atlantic, under terrible danger, and had been posted to the Pacific to rest. His fellow officers did not support him, as they should. His *team* failed – no matter how hard he tried to make it succeed. This understanding never occurred to me during multiple readings of the novel. I kept returning to the book to find out why it was considered one of the great ones. The perspective on the Captain had to be explained to me and only then did appreciation erupt.

Conclusion

You have seen a little of the value of reading and of the many choices available. What about the question of where do you get the time to read more? Here are three of the many ways: The first, use what time you have. There are many opportunities; seize them and make them habits. Read in the bathroom, over your breakfast, or during your commute. Watch less TV. Have you ever waited on a line? You get the point.

A less obvious way to read is to have the material read to you. This is often called *books-on-tape*, though the *tape* could be any of a variety of media. While driving your car, doing errands, exercising, or working around the yard or house you can be enjoying a great story. Much is available to you and the habit can be addicting. Lastly, learn to speed-read. Based upon the premise that you are smart and capable of assimilating more than one word at a time, this will move you from looking at text a phrase at a time to scanning it a line at a time. The improvements in your speed are substantial.

There are other techniques for processing materials faster. Consider the need to understand a technology book. Begin with the table of contents. There might be a single chapter that fulfills your need. Next, page through the entire book, quickly. Get a sense of the book: its layout, whether chapters have summaries, have graphs or pictures. You can now read the first and last paragraphs of the most critical chapters before reading more. The techniques of *skimming* are very real. Use them, as they will help you to go over important information several times, quickly.

Take notes as you read. They will help you comprehend, analyze, and retain information. You might use yellow highlighters (and the many other colors that are available). There are even new products that do the same thing but save you from the perceived crime of marking up a book. Try a Kindle or an iPad. These new tools can make reading even more fun and easier to do.

Chapter 6 – WRITE BETTER

Three Simple Rules

My first memory of anyone trying to teach me to write was formed back in Saint Agatha's elementary school. Sister Mary told each of us – and I still remember her words – "had to identify our theme." What was a theme? Why didn't I just raise my hand to ask the question? Perhaps everyone knew the answer, and so my logic was that of Solomon's proverb: "Better to remain silent and be thought a fool, than to open your mouth and remove all doubt." How old was I, eight or ten?

Years later, I finally understood her lesson. She was telling us that we had to pick what we were going to write about: our summer vacation, an opinion on something, or what happened in the (fill in the blank).

This lesson, understood so much later, is important when writing.

Rule #1: Know what you are writing about!

Ok. Got it, you think. Stupid but, yes, the rule makes sense. So what is next?

Rule #2: Write it!

That's it? Isn't there more? Yes, there is one additional rule.

Rule #3: Rewrite it, over and over (also known as edit forever).

That's it. You now know about writing. The above three rules are not a surprise if you learned them early and have practiced them often. That might not be the case, particularly with Rule #1, #2, and #3 – wait, that's all of them! Too many people don't know what they are writing about, don't write it, and certainly don't work at making it better!

This is not a criticism of the average *wannabe* author. Consider just the first rule and think of *Gone with the Wind*. What is the book about? Is it a love story between Scarlett and Rhett; a tale of the Civil War; one of Scarlett's growth; or all of the preceding? The greatness of that book is that it achieves each of them, virtually perfectly.

Even if you are clear on what you are writing about, how do you achieve the goal you have set? If what you are writing is meant to persuade, to deal with painful issues as a note of consolation, or just to be a humorous story, how do you do it? None of those things are easy.

 One of the great secrets about writing is: *To do it well is hard work!* There is a story about a great author's greatest ending – something re-written and polished a hundred times. Near the end of his life he still regretted feeling rushed by the publisher. He felt that he did not take enough time to get it right. The nasty secret that underlies writing is that it is very much about re-writing. Mrs. Tolstoy copied the entire 900 page novel, *War and Peace*, some dozen times – by hand – as her husband, Leo, kept changing it.

There is another secret, and that is that *there is no single way to write well.* Some authors sketch out everything in advance; others will tell you that they "have to finish the book to learn how it comes out." Margaret

Mitchell, the author of *Gone with the Wind* wrote the ending first, then began at the beginning working toward the famous line, "Frankly, Scarlett, I don't give a damn!"

Some Simple Suggestions

There are things you can do to improve your writing skills, whether your intent is to write faster, more comprehensively, more effectively – or just for fun. Here are a few in no particular priority, without any pretence that they are all-encompassing. There are others, too, including your own. Use them and your writing will get better, and that's a promise!

Make a list. Just put down words (or phrases) that you feel should be included in what you are writing. Be sloppy. Brainstorm. A trick is to put them on small pieces of paper, which can be moved around, grouped, and regrouped. Later on you can put them into the order that makes sense to you: priority, time, person, cost – whatever.

Some of the ideas that you put down will, upon second viewing, clearly be *details* subordinate to *categories*. That's fine. Add more; delete what is unneeded or redundant. A rule-of-thumb is to have about seven categories with an equal number of details for each. It is fine to have fewer; for example, you might write that "you have three things to say..." When you get too many – "I have twenty nine things to say..." – you might want to consolidate them. Readers find that a structure helps them assimilate things.

One list of categories often used is: Who, What, Where, When, Why, How, and How Much? Try this generic collection; they are a good starting point.

Write. Start at the top of the page. Your goal is to reach the end of your piece so that you can begin the re-write. If you already have a list, fine, just begin to write. If you don't intend to have one – and many writers do not use them – begin anyway. The first question you may have is "what is the first word to write," or its slightly larger brother, "...first sentence?" It does not matter. It is important to avoid the *getting stuck on the first line* syndrome. Write a second sentence, then a third. They don't even have to follow each other logically. You may even write beginning in the middle. Your list and its details allow you to start with one, adding others later.

Don't worry about grammar or spelling for now. Write until you are finished. You then have a *complete* piece. Are you missing things? Would you like to change their order? Do you need to expand some of the points? Are some things redundant or confusing? The answer to all of these questions will almost always be YES!

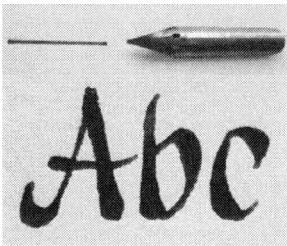

Of course, and the importance of this cannot be minimized, *do you know what you want to write?* Note how this contrasts with Rule #1 (Decide what you are writing about). You may be clear that you are writing an opinion, but not know exactly what your opinion is. Often the act of writing is used to clarify thoughts. As you clarify your writing, let the writing clarify your thoughts and ideas.

Now edit, using some of the techniques that follow – and find others of your own.

Look at what you've written. Your complete piece is in front of you. Before looking at any detail, consider the whole thing. Is it too long or too short? Does it start by telling the reader what you are writing about; or is it a mystery, to be revealed at the end? Both techniques are appropriate, depending on what you want. Are you happy with the amount of time, space, or words you wrote in each section? Is there a beginning, middle, and an end? These, and more, are considerations only you can determine.

Move things around. Particular words you have written may be colorful, articulate, or even perfect; the thought may be exactly what you want to convey – but not where it is. You can *cut and paste* and change location. One of the great advantages of word-processors is that it takes mere seconds to move text to another location. Your writing should have logical groupings. Each paragraph should convey consistent points.

The words matter. Good writing has to have substance – like a movie plot – but the dialogue is important too, and this is made up of words. You have a huge choice of vocabulary. Words have meanings and can convey images and even feelings. Was the steam hot or scalding? You might also consider whether (and how many) descriptive words to use. Did they kiss, or kiss passionately? It is fun to find the right words. Dictionaries and thesauruses help and are available in word-processors.

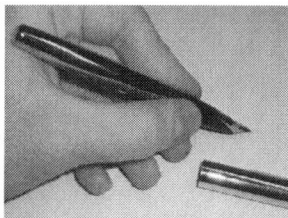

Spelling, punctuation, and grammar matter. Check your grammar. Guides such as the short *The Elements of Style* by Strunk & White teach some of the rules of English. While it is very important that your final product is grammatically correct and contains no spelling errors, don't obsess over this. You need not structure your writing so that it will be considered a masterpiece of English grammar. The subtleties of proper grammar can be complex. You need only make your work understandable to your expected audience. There are obvious pitfalls to avoid, however. Here are a few of the most common:

- ✓ Know the difference between:
  - ➢ there, their and they're
  - ➢ your and you're
  - ➢ its and it's
  - ➢ then and than
  - ➢ who's and whose
  - ➢ past and passed
  - ➢ affect and effect
  - ➢ beside and besides

- ✓ Don't overuse punctuation. If you're not too familiar with the proper use of semicolons for example, avoid them. Don't overuse commas. They should only be placed where they are needed to make clear the meaning and flow of the sentence.
- ✓ Give your reader a chance to breathe. Sentences should express a single thought and not run on forever.
- ✓ Make sure your sentences have at least one subject and one verb.
- ✓ Remember to use your apostrophes correctly. Plurals get an *s* where possessives get an *apostrophe s* and possessive plurals get an *s apostrophe*.

✓ Watch out for double negatives; they will reverse your meaning.

Get critique.   Get an outside opinion of what you have written. Even though you know what you *want* to say, there is no guaranty that *what you have written conveys the information you wish it to.* Getting a valid opinion, though, is hard. Who do you ask? Asking your mother usually elicits the enthusiastic response "It is wonderful, my brilliant...!" and no disrespect to any mother is intended here.   A friend may provide comments, but usually not; after all, that is how they remain your friend. It may take some effort to find a useful critic – so avoid abusing that person by constantly asking about every one of your edited versions.

Useful feedback can be hard to accept. Your words become akin to your children – and no one ever wants to hear that their children are ugly! Were you told that a sentence or a paragraph was difficult to understand? Was the reader deliberately lying?   Know that some feedback may not be valid.   The author has the responsibility and the power to change or let stay the words in the work. What to do is your choice.

Be interesting; don't be boring.   Variety is the spice of life, so mix up your writing. Vary the sentence lengths, the way sentences start, the words used. Thesauruses exist to show the very many alternative ways of saying things. Use them. Some books build toward a climax while others begin at the end of the story. Sometimes the hero lives; the couple lives happily ever after, other times, not. Informative pieces can be amusing and colorful, or state "just the facts, ma'am." Be different, and consider being surprising.

Be aware of your audience. Who will be reading your work? What are their expectations, their backgrounds, their biases? Will your audience be school children or college professors? The reader needs to be *managed*. Ensure that a point that you've made can truly be grasped by an unsuspecting reader. Make paragraphs flow with each pointing to the next. Know why you are writing: to entertain, persuade, motivate, or excuse. Make that purpose clear.

Tell them, tell them, and then tell them again. You may want to tell the audience of your premise early and clearly. You may later spend the bulk of your effort in showing the details that provide the foundation upon which everything stands. End with a conclusion that summarizes, restates, and is memorable.

Clarify. There is no single right way to write (would "no single correct way to write" be: better, more correct, more desirable…, or simply, *betterer*?) But some of these above rules-of-thumb will help purge bad tendencies and wrong writing (poor writing?). Simplicity is usually best, but nuance can be beautiful, as is making the words flow, rhyme, or strike with power. But some authors polish and polish and get the piece to the point where the message is impenetrable, or even worse, lost – that happens too often. Clarity matters! This point can be confirmed by reading virtually any of recent Laws. You read them again and again and are still not sure what they mean.

Conclusion

Much can be seen of you from how you write. In your writings are found evidence of your ability, creativity, and understanding of issues. Professionally, writing well will help you achieve a goal, set a direction, or change an opinion. It is important to write well – but u no dat. Personal writing can expose your soul in love letters, ones of sympathy or of joy.

Writing can also be fun. Keep a diary. Send letters to new-born members of your family (the mother will keep them and the child will always treasure you for having written to them all their lives). Pen a family story – they get lost as the generations pass. It does not matter what you write, just do so. Practice really does make perfect. Creating a *body of work* begins with the first piece. Larry Brown, a Mississippi author and firefighter, noted that his goal was not to write a single story, but many; and that after you have written a thousand stories, you will have learned how to write them better.

It is not unreasonable to point out that you do have a thousand tales in your portfolio waiting to be written.

Chapter 7 – CREATE BETTER

Too few believe they are creative. This is sad. You are and can easily make yourself more so. Any thought to the contrary is pernicious, mendacious, and just flat-out wrong.

Those who believe they are *not,* think that creativity just happens. This insidious belief can become a prescription for failure, a self-fulfilling prophecy. Spontaneous creativity certainly does happen – it is amazing how many lightning bolts arrive daily – but creativity is most often the result of the disciplined pursuit of a purpose, that is, plain hard work. Most *Eureka*! moments arrive after much time and effort. Forgotten in the glow of success were the thousands of failed experiments before the dawn of the light bulb.

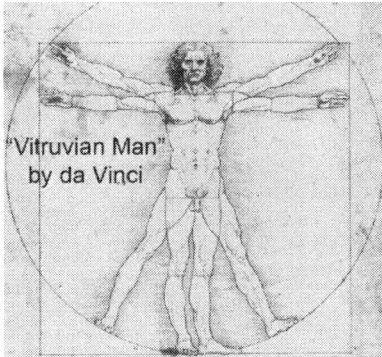
"Vitruvian Man" by da Vinci

Those who succeed, irrespective of their avocation, often describe a common success *trick*. The legendary golfer, Gary Player, and the archetypical Hollywood mogul, Samuel Goldwin both said, "The harder I work, the luckier I get." Thomas Alva Edison, perhaps history's most prolific inventor, put it similarly, though differently: "Genius is 1% inspiration and 99% perspiration."

So let's go to work so you can become more creative.

The Definition of Creativity

According to Webster: "1: The quality of being creative 2: the ability to create"

That does not seem to help, so let's examine the definition of *creative*:

"1: Marked by the ability or power to create; given to creating; 2: Productive; 3: Having the quality of something created rather than imitated: imaginative"

There are now hints with power, ability, imagination, and productivity being elements. Let's keep working and look up *create*:

"1: to bring into existence; 2a: to invest with a new form, office, or rank; b: to produce or bring about a new course of action; 3: to cause occasion; 4a: to produce through imaginative skill; b: design. The synonym of create is design."

This definition provides meat, particularly the words, "to bring into existence."

Creativity's Source

For believers, the greatest example of this is the *Creation*, so God is the ultimate source of creativity. For

"The Creation of Man" by Michelangelo

atheists, all of creation came from the *Big Bang,* with creativity the result of whatever random things that were set in motion then. It is not possible to teach how to achieve being "Touched by the hand of God" other than espousing the path of prayer, doing good works, etc.; nor how to impact a past random chain of events to affect events today.

We assume the human mind is the source of creativity. The brain is by far the greatest of all computers. It has been the subject of wonder and experiment for millennia – but is still a mystery today. There are, however, a few things about *wisdom's seat* that you should know.

The mind digests: Information is the food of the mind. Keep it well-fed both in quality and quantity. *Learning* is the successful feeding of the mind. *Research* is the deliberate acquisition of subject-specific information. The more research performed and the more information collected, the better fed your mind will be. Of course, you can feed it junk. It is your choice.

The mind processes: Thinking is another name for this processing whether done consciously or subconsciously. Thoughts are born, as are ideas. The subconscious will also yield vague feelings, sometimes referred to as intuition to those who listen to themselves.

The mind orders: Information is created by examining, filtering, and sorting data. Information can also be found in data about data, i.e. *metadata*. Your mind is ideally suited to finding patterns, doing so in many ways, including comparisons: *this*, as opposed to *that*.

The mind learns: It absorbs facts. It also forecasts the future from the past. This is called experience. This information can be about what works or does not. Edison learned many, many ways how not to make a light bulb. Called the best teacher, experience can be gotten deliberately through experimentation.

The mind builds: Often the combination of data yields new information. This is like the creation of a cathedral from individual stones, where the sum of the parts is greater than the individual pieces together. The power of the individual mind is incredible and can be augmented by other individual's input.

Actions and Attitudes

There are also actions and attitudes to make you more creative and more successful in your pursuits.

Be positive! It is important to always seek the affirmative rather than the negative. Always provide positive support for your endeavors. Beware the *experienced* voice who cries "It failed the last time!" or "This is the way it's always been done!"

Related to this is the dictum "No idea is wrong!" Any idea that can be generated may help you, but don't get side-tracked by any one idea. Create a lot of them whether you are alone or working as part of a team. Quashing any suggestion has the effect of removing a mind from the group. The best idea should bloom as a result of the synergistic effects of a group's shared mind. Many factors conspire to wilt potentially successful thoughts. The "it won't work" attitude – lack of confidence whispers – can doom any useful thought.

Assume success; you are more likely to win, otherwise, to fail. Which would you prefer?

Take a careful look. When all else fails, read the directions. This old witticism masks a sad fact: Often, reality is ignored. This may be the result

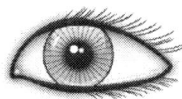

of familiarity, boredom, or carelessness.

Always consider the situation, problem, or item as it exists. Describe it as whatever makes sense or by: who, what, where, when, why, how, how much. Ensure that you fully understand the *current state* before proceeding. Humanity has an astounding and sometimes blinding capacity to self-delude; keep your eyes and mind open to reality.

Break the rules and ask. Columbus was asked to stand an egg on its end. He did so by crushing one end of the egg. "Everything is fair, once you have done it."

There are always guidelines, assumptions, and rules that can be followed. But they may not apply or may no longer be valid. The environment might have changed; the guidelines become irrelevant; the assumptions, specious.

You will only find out their validity when carefully considering each.

There are two magic words that can help promote creativity. They are better known than "It was a dark and stormy night," the beginning words of Snoopy's novel (originally from a notoriously clichéd Edward Bulwer-Lytton novel). Unfortunately, these two magic words are too often not used enough.

"What if…" are two great words to begin the search for an answer. Pose a variety of questions. Make many leaps. Take anything and ask *what if* it was not true. Whenever an obstacle or constraint is found, repeat the incantation "What if…"

Choose brilliance. Ordinary people can act in extraordinary ways. Brilliance can be a choice. But there is a problem. While it is generally understood that humans use only a fraction of their brain power, most do not believe that they are capable of doing more. There are many companies, teams and individuals who deliver on their potential. That is either because these people are "the best of the best" or, more commonly, that they believed in themselves and chose to pay the price to succeed.

Success breeds success. While hoping to win the lottery might be an interesting strategy, making a conscious choice to do and achieve is a better one. Make it a habit to do the smart thing, where the adjective *smart* does not simply refer to the short-term or expedient. Choose to act from the big-picture perspective. While short-term gains may be a necessary, long-term success should be the goal.

Seek opportunity. "There are no problems, only opportunities," is an old business axiom. This has a core of truth. Turning problems into opportunities changes the way you think. Of course, sometimes you have to deal with problems that are really, well, problems. However, the point of this axiom is to start with the premise that, whatever the cause, you should choose to make the best of a bad situation by turning it into gold.

The fall of Constantinople in 1453 ended a thousand years of history. It closed the Silk Road which linked Europe to Asia – a problem. But it gave impetus to the age of discovery. Columbus sailed across a dark ocean to find a new route to China. He failed to reach China but did find a new continent – gold!

The work invested in reaping the benefits offered by an opportunity will potentially offset the negative impact of the original problem. Two psychological factors are in play here: the energizing effect from the pursuit of gain; and benefits gained from a change of perspective – the new view. This energizing effect and change of perspective can only help enhance your ability to solve the original problem.

Always keep an eye out for a potential opportunity. Whether resulting from a problem-turned-benefit or simply appearing unexpectedly, they are always around the next corner.

Forget what is known. The bumble bee cannot fly. Its structure is aerodynamically unsound. It has a fat body and small wings and thus cannot lift off. This has been proven by numerous engineers.

This example illustrates an important point. The bee, of course, does not know what it cannot do. It just goes about its business – flying from the hive to the many plants where it gathers nectar while fertilizing them. The bee is a visual and aural part of a lazy summer day and is key in the propagation of life – because it *does* fly!

What is known might just be wrong.

Accept new ideas. It is essential that openness be maintained. Examine and critique. Don't assume. Be prepared to learn, to explore the unknown. Don't let the problem, the plan, or the solution be pre-determined. While it is true that "If you don't know where you are going, any road will take you there." it is more so that "Surprises lie just around every corner." Keep your eyes and mind open to new ideas.

This fundamental attitude is essential to getting the most value from the effort expended in research and in data gathering. Ask *open-ended questions* – ones that allow unexpected responses. This is in contrast to closed-ended questions which have few possible answers. For example, an open-ended question would be: Why do you like your car? In contrast, a closed-ended questions would be: Do you own a car? Open-ended questions do not confine the answerer to a predefined set of possible answers. They allow him/her to formulate a response in any way he/she sees fit, which fosters a free-flow of information. They expand the solution space, cause a reexamination of assumptions, and can achieve a new perspective.

There is comfort in being an expert – in knowing what we know. The new contains risks. Willingness to accept new ideas requires courage. Columbus faced the known certainty of sailing over the edge of the world to discover a new one. Yet, he pursued his dream.

Be willing and prepared to sail your ship beyond the known.

Have fun. While it may be true that "Necessity is the mother of invention," where is it written that the process of inventing should not be enjoyable? Inventing, or creating can be hard work. But actively working to create a fun environment has a number of psychological benefits that further the pursuit of the objective. Enjoyment of an activity increases the desire to pursue it. It bridges barriers, builds teams, and eases conflicts. Playfulness, the mark of a child, represents a state of relaxation – a lack of tension – and helps you digest new experiences while encouraging experimentation.

Each person or group will have its own character and will find humor in unique ways. Don't forget to deliberately encourage the spontaneous.

Trust yourself. It is so easy to find an answer in a book or to be given one by the wise. It is much harder to create from scratch.

Each individual, as well as any group, needs to respect their own abilities; to recognize the degree of competence they have. The individual's experience and the collective skills of the group have great value in crafting a solution. Trust in your abilities to create a good solution.

The creative idea may be manifest in either the *BIG idea* or just a thought. Give credence to intuition's *little voice* in your ear. It is real. It represents the subconscious presenting the results of the mind's background processing of all the data and information it has received.

Ideas voiced can be heard and remembered.

Be a warrior. The ideas and attitudes outlined here (and the many others which will later be presented) are intended for use, i.e., they are tools in a workbox. The job may be large like building the Panama Canal across a mountainous isthmus or the Suez across the forbidding desert. These challenges are not easily faced but, if overcome, have the potential to reshape the world. Creativity matters.

The most famous of the Jedi warriors was three-feet tall and green. His name was Yoda. His words clearly explain the philosophy of achievement: "There is no try, only do, or do not."

Ask what the risks and benefits are of inaction, of failure and of success. Risks can be monetary, political, and even to life itself. Your goal is to advance. You must be prepared to do so aggressively and tenaciously.

After the second Battle of the Wilderness during the American Civil War, the Union Army had suffered over 17,000 casualties. General Grant demonstrated how he differed from his predecessor. Everyone assumed that he would order retreat. He did the opposite, tenaciously pursuing General Lee's army until a final victory was won.

The challenge is ahead. Overcome it, go under it, or go around it. Just move forward.

Grow your imagination. There is virtually nothing in this world that cannot be done better with practice. That is true equally for swinging a hammer, cooking a dinner, and for reinventing a business.

The pursuit of imagination should not be left behind in childhood and forgotten. Make it part of each day. One of the explicit activities of yours and your team should be to exercise the mind. Consider common things and let your mind wander off the page. For example, "What is a dot?" It could be the top of a pole from a thousand feet up; an owl's eye; or a distant planet to Galileo. There are many creative exercises that you can use to warm up the creative juices, exactly as oil needs to be warmed up in a racecar engine.

Science has shown that long-term dream deprivation can cause insanity. But you do not only dream while you sleep. It happens spontaneously. Albert Einstein was famous for his *thought experiments*. He would often think through his ideas by running virtual experiments in his mind. This is akin to directed daydreaming. You should occasionally, and intentionally, allow your mind to dream while awake – daydream. This exercise will enhance your innate imagination and creativity – skills that you nurtured in childhood but may atrophy due to disuse.

Skills unused are often lost. Exercise dreaming.

Look for the possibilities of combination. The 26 letters in the English alphabet can be arranged into the works of Shakespeare, Biblical psalms, or even pornography. The 88 keys on a piano were used to compose Bach's "Well-Tempered Clavier," Ellington's "Take the 'A' Train," and the Beach Boys' "California Girls." Individually, each of the characters or notes is so small. That size masks enormous depth and power.

Stepping stones chained together form a path. They may, however, require – as the characters of the alphabet and notes of the keyboard – specific arrangement. Answers to your questions may require _some assembly_, too. Three rocks – red, grey, and black – can be used to form a path or a wall. They can also be combined for other purposes. If one is iron ore, another limestone, and the third coal, they can together form steel – sword blades and girders – weapons of war and great cities.

Deliberately consider how it is possible to make progress in small increments – every trip begins with a single step – the pursuit of the _BIG idea_ may obfuscate the progress made in small increments.

Synergy is where combinations yield more than the sum of the parts. Synergies can develop from unexpected combinations – look for them. Find elements that foster growth of others. Components of beauty might not, themselves, be beautiful – but remain essential nevertheless.

Water, light, and dirt – combined with a seed – can create life.

Find a second way. Solving a problem or identifying a path toward reaping the benefits of a new opportunity might only represent the first step. The initial answer may only point in a direction. Other approaches – ones that might be faster, cheaper, easier, or just plain better – may be there for the taking.

Alternatives may include short, medium, and long-term ones or comprehensive vs. point solutions. If you are part of a group, consider splitting into teams – each one charged with morphing the solution. There are always options.

An author once instructed that instead of writing: "As I write this, it is raining," try "The water is coursing down the windowpanes, joining the many small rivulets…" Even better, "I am looking out of the window at the rain drops pelting the lilac bush on the front yard where we hid from mom when she was mad…"

Make trying again a habit.

What would _____ say or do? A curious strength becomes available with role-playing. Wearing another's identity opens a different universe of knowledge, action, and thought. Where it was once difficult to see, a change in perspective can clear the fog and bring into focus a more compelling solution. His, her, or their perspective may be just what is needed.

This exercise can be done by yourself or as a group. Choose to be someone or some group. Review their world and attitudes. What might they need; what experiences might they bring? What are their strengths and weaknesses? Now to the question: Look through the eyes of the president, or the richest man on Earth, or Leonardo da Vinci. Their eyes would see things differently but they're not here. Whatever is thus envisioned is the direct result of some new, creative power unleashed.

Children play pretend. Do so, too.

See the Result. John Forbes Nash won the Nobel Prize for Economics for work that influences the world in many ways. He is considered one of the great minds in history. A distinguishing mark of many of his discoveries was that he seemed to have the ability to envision the answer. It was often later, perhaps over a period of years, that he was able to complete the work necessary to lay out all the steps needed to prove that his vision was accurate. He saw the result by overlooking the immediate difficulties obstructing the path forward.

Psychologists have noted that solutions are often visualized first. Einstein realized that the feeling one gets while being pulled to earth is identical to that one gets while accelerating. He thus stated that since gravity and acceleration seem the same, they are the same. Nine years of work with the help of the mathematician Marcel Grossmann were needed to develop the mathematics behind the general Theory of Relativity. This *result* of his then changed the world's conception of time and space.

If you can see the end, work toward it.

Write it down. History is filled with discoveries, once known, that were forgotten. Civilizations and cities; ideas and concepts; kings and heroes – rule, disappear, and are rediscovered. Everyone is busy. This is a trap. This *busy-ness* causes a focus on the present rather than the future; on the details rather than on the mosaic; on the action rather than the plan.

Write ideas down. Don't let a good idea be forgotten. They can be added to by another; the first idea may only be a step in the right direction. Carry a piece of paper – a notebook with pencil. Take the very few seconds to jot thoughts down, draw a picture or a graph. .

With ideas assembled, they can be prioritized, grouped, shared, and grown. The first step towards the realization of an idea is seeing it.

See what has been thought.

Use the resources available.   There are many obstacles to progress but also resources aplenty to support you. Just take advantage of them – and why wouldn't you?

An Internet search on virtually any topic will deliver tens, if not thousands of potential resources associated with the topic. There is information and experts. Special interest groups often exist.

Other resources available include high-speed global communication links; modern engineered materials not previously available (plastics, ceramics, laminates, etc); and three-dimension graphic visualization tools.

Another type of oft-forgotten resource includes solutions tried, failed, and successful – throughout history – in other fields and endeavors. Remember to search for similar activities which may have occurred in the past. Learn from their mistakes and successes. There is no need to reinvent the wheel.

Friends, colleagues, and professors can assist on virtually any pursuit – if even only to suggest alternate paths to follow.

Isaac Newton saw further because he "stood on the shoulders of giants." So can you.

Use Teams.   A special instance of the above instruction to *use resources* is the creation of a team.

They are powerful, bringing together the sum total of their life experiences. Together, they embody a staggeringly large number of situations that they have encountered over the years. Teams create synergy – where two plus two can equal fifty-five!

The challenge is to tap into that pool of expertise. You want people to cooperate, to become invested in your purpose, and to leverage each other's strengths.

One of the most popular ways to do this is to *Brainstorm,* a technique developed by Alex Osborn of advertising industry fame. He believed that, while it is true that some great ideas *pop into one's head*, more often they arise as a result of an enormous amount of work. He felt that the technique of brainstorming was not a substitute for effort. Rather it is a different way of working. The concept is to take individual's thoughts and ideas and share them with the *group mind*. Each member of the team can then use others' ideas to create new ones.

Forming a team can be totally haphazard or done after careful consideration. Usually it is best to limit its size to no more than a dozen or so. Appoint a leader to enforce the rules, keep focus, and prevent any voice from dominating. This role is important and must be agreed to by all.

Tell the team, in advance, what the goal is. Give them background material. Don't assume that a miracle will happen all by itself. Smart people are that way because they work at it.

The actual brainstorming session can take place using a variety of techniques. Their selection can be part of the team-building exercise. Make sure that everyone is comfortable.

Techniques include: 1) Warm-ups at the beginning: Ask what a smell weighs or how many piano-tuners there are in NYC. Make sure you get everyone involved. 2) The five-minute drill: Everyone writes one word or idea on a Post-It. When time is up, put them on the walls for all to see. 3) *Association* can uncover new vistas. One idea is used to generate the next, and so on. Random ideas are put aside for later consideration. Write all the ideas down as they are generated.

You then sort them into *categories*. Where one category is lacking in volume, ask whether it should be expanded. Are categories missing? Note that you have just entered the world of *metadata*, data about data. It can be useful and provide an additional perspective to you.

This word, *perspective* is a useful one. Often ideas occur when a situation is looked at differently. The apple falling from a tree inspired Newton's thought that the Moon is falling – it is. Here is another perspective. Have each person take 5 minutes to draw the problem, its elements, and their solution. Laugh at their lack of artistic talents as they present the drawings to each other. Does each capture the situation in the same way? – Probably not.

There are many such techniques to use. Invent some yourself. Be creative.

Conclusion

It is not cynical to truly believe that it is possible to be more creative by performing some simple actions and adopting the right attitudes – almost pulling creativity out of a box on demand.

This chapter may not transform you to the level of creativity that history remembers — but it might. It will certainly increase your ability to be creative. All that you have to do is — do — and you can!

Chapter 8 – ANALYZE BETTER

The layman may say "what the heck?" While an engineer might say "...we need to perform an analysis." If all goes well after some thought, investigation, or consultation, you might hear "got it" or "the analysis has determined that..." For the very fortunate, they may proclaim "it was satisfying, or amazing, or fun!" Finding out what is behind the curtain (remember the Wizard of Oz) can provide an "A-ha!" moment that will be long-remembered.

Try dropping a plate onto a marble floor. It will break. We're sorry this happened (particularly if it was an expensive plate and you were blindly following our instructions). Analysis might be thought of as what you do when the situation is a bit more complicated than that; simply stated, *analysis* is: "the process of identifying a cause for an effect."

People have been trying to develop a well-defined method for doing so for thousands of years and have come up with many. They're referred to as *analysis systems*. Plato's great student, Aristotle, thought that four things had to be considered: the matter from which the item is made; what it is intended to be; who shaped it;

Aristotle

and finally, what it actually becomes. For believers in Karma, a person chooses between good or evil; God then arranges everything that follows. In the philosophy of Determinism, the universe is a chain of causes and effects eventually leading to the belief that there is no free will at all.

Analysis is performed on situations, systems, or the way people think. There are technical analyses which can be performed on chemical, electrical, and even information systems. They can be performed on business markets, operations, and stock prices which attempt to discern the future based on the past. An important type of analysis performed by the military is called *battlefield situation analysis*. For each of these, and for many more, the tools of analysis have become more and more specialized and sophisticated.

Analysis matters, but making decisions based on it matters more. Two thousand years ago Plato remarked: "A good decision is based on knowledge and not on numbers." It is analysis that gets you from confronting a mystery by having some information to eventually reaching an understanding which is knowledge.

You were probably never taught to *do analysis*. How is this possible? Analysis is a critical skill – something everyone needs to do all the time. It is something applicable to almost every aspect of your life. Without analysis you are reduced to *flying blind* or, at best, relying on *gut-feel* and both of these are woefully inadequate.

Regardless of all the many types of analyses available, the most important one to you is the one that addresses your own personal needs. This chapter will give you both a practical understanding and some *how to's*. These will help you immediately. They will also make you more confident as you move forward. Having these tools in your quiver will make you a more powerful hunter, in this case, of the truth. You can then better choose what to do.

Basics

Webster's dictionary starts with an eight-word definition of *analysis*: "separation of a whole into its component parts." We expand upon this just a bit by adding the reason for doing so: that analysis is the process of taking something apart to its pieces *in order to increase your understanding of the whole.* This modified definition holds true for all analyses. What changes are the mechanics of disassembly: a mechanic taking apart a car engine which is leaking oil; an engineer dissecting a system that failed to properly calculate the data; or a supervisor speaking with each employee of a factory to determine why productivity has decreased. Though the details of the disassembly differ, the process is one of identifying and examining the parts.

The goal is understanding. To get this, you need to see the parts, how they relate and a lot more. This comes from the *analysis questions*. These you have known all your life, but have you ever been told that they are part of a process?

The analysis questions' simplicity could be considered embarrassing; indeed, they are almost laughable. But, as part of a process – a system for analysis – they are incredibly powerful. But you know this, as you know each of these seven questions by heart:

Who? What? Where? When? Why? How? How Much?

So what were you expecting, that you could not do analysis? Don't you believe in yourself by now, understanding that you were smarter than you knew, perhaps lacking only some information at times? Analysis is the gathering of information needed to answer questions, targeted on a specific circumstance, in a systematic fashion. Most of the time, analysis is done by asking these questions – making sure to get and consider carefully their answers – then, drilling down to ask additional ones. Systematically considering these additional questions – and discarding many – provides the basis of the next level of analysis.

Just for fun, let's take one situation and do an analysis of it, illustrating how some of the questions might be answered. Let's briefly look at Communism in Cuba which, like its mentor-state, the former Soviet Union, has failed in its promise to its people. The question you might pose for analysis is: "Why did Cuban Communism fail? This is a complex topic so let's see how our seven questions do...

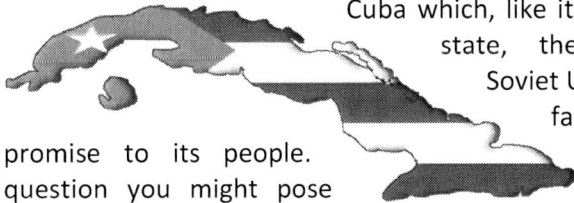

Who? We believe that people matter more than anything, so any analysis should begin with a consideration of them. Who is affected by Communism in Cuba? One answer is "Everyone in the country." But other *who* questions might help provide additional insight. Who is the head of the Government? Raul Castro, Cuba's former Minister of Defense. Who was in charge before him? His brother, Fidel, was in charge for some 40 years. Wow, this country is being run almost like a family business, so you may ask: Are there other members of the family involved? A little research will determine that Raul's son-in-law is the head of GAESA, the armed forces holding company which by his admission, runs over 40% of Cuba's economy...and so it goes.

The questions could continue, with each answer sparking others. Does this say that the people who control the guns are making most of the money in Cuba?

What? ...is Communism? It is a type of economic system and form of government in which everyone works for, and only for, the State. There are no other jobs. You cannot legally cut someone else's hair and charge for it. In a pure Communist system, everyone is a member of the State, which takes care of everything for everyone else. This might explain how so many people believed so deeply and so early in the revolutions that created communist states. Certainly the idea that people have to take care of each other is a powerful one – echoing Christian belief. Communism shares some other things with religion – but not God. Some consider the Communist Government to be a form of Deity.

In 2010, Cuba announced that it was going to lay off 500,000 people. Since it is illegal to work outside the government, a list of *private jobs* was also published to accommodate the flood of unemployed. Slightly more than 100 approved occupations were listed, including working as a: wedding photographer, flower salesperson, or as a fancy-dress dancer (required to wear a costume styled after a 1940's Cuban singer, Beny More – you can't make this up)!

Why? ...did Communism arrive in Cuba? Because in the 1950's, the Soviet Union's Government sought to extend its domination over the Earth during the Cold War. They helped fund a young revolutionary, Fidel Castro, to overthrow the previous corrupt

Fidel Castro

government. Fidel's message was that Communism's egalitarianism would ensure that there would be no rich, nor poor – everyone would be equal – a powerful inducement to the poor.

Where? Cuba is just 90 miles off the coast of the United States. This geographic consideration made it a strategic asset for the Soviets. Cuba was both a gateway to the Americas and a base for potential offensive operations against the US, comparable to the missile bases the U.S. had placed at the edges of the USSR.

When? The 20th century was the time for Communism's grand experiment. Injected into Russia by the Germans during the First World War, it bankrupted the USSR, but not before being spread to many other countries. Four remain: China, which is now trying desperately to convert to a Capitalist System while leaving all power in the Communist Government's hands; Vietnam, which is doing the same but beginning as one of the poorest countries on the planet; North Korea, which is by all accounts, run by a government-run-amok and whose people are suffering greatly; and Cuba, which, in 2010 began following the path being attempted by the first two.

There might be other questions of time: what happens as it passes and the Castro Brothers continue to grow older? What about the Cuban population as it grays – how will their pensions get paid? and more…

How? …does the economy actually work in a Communist Country? Since there are no competitive pressures within the nation to incentivize any improvements, history shows us that answer is: not well! The economy is centrally planned with 5-year plans and written quotas. Anecdotes describe the reaction to these: televisions having screws driven in by hammers; making ten-thousand left, size 7, black shoes which were reported as 5,000 pairs of shoes; and plowing soil a quarter of an inch deep while driving a tractor at top speed – none of which increase quality, but all do act to achieve the imposed quotas.

The System begins with the young receiving not just subject-matter education but indoctrination extolling the State (and censorship applied to hide any view of alternative-systems' standard of living). The State chooses professions, so behind-the-scenes influences are highly sought out. Later, this has developed into the power of commissars fostering corruption and a vast black-market economy. In the official economy, there is no incentive to work hard; highly bloated staffing levels exist. All this drains money that could be used as investment so the economy falls further behind others.

How Much? ...do Cubans earn? It is estimated that the average wage on the island is $20-$30 per month at the unofficial exchange rate excluding the massive subsidies for education, transport, and healthcare. But as the government runs out of money, the question of how they will pay these subsidies must be troubling to the Castros.

From our coarse example above, you get a sense of the power of our seven analysis questions and also of the fun you can have in applying them to so many problems. After satisfying yourself that you've answered all of the questions you could think to ask, you would review all of the information to determine a solution to the original problem: "Why did Cuban Communism fail?"

We note, again, the value of writing down questions and answers especially when there are many, and of prioritizing them, and of how analysis takes effort to uncover the truth. Applied to your own specific concerns, the work involved will pay you back many times.

More Advanced Analysis

Structured Analysis takes the seven questions to a next level of formality breaking areas down to their components and adding rigor to the work to be performed. This might include: what *is* the information; how does it flow; what exactly does each piece of information mean; what are the processes; what are the inputs and outputs to each component (priorities, money, anything)? Note that the formal listing of all of these items is a part of the analysis, too.

Root Cause Analysis is often done after a problem has occurred. RCA is based on the idea that there is one primary cause to explain why something happened. It is intended as a way to find and fundamentally fix rather than just dealing with the aftermath. It describes cause and effect sequentially. There are multiple techniques for doing this including drawing a *tree's root* which starts with the problem and describes the various factors that may have led to it. The root-system expands, level upon level, until one *Root Cause* is identified.

For example, say your car's dashboard trim piece fell off. Why? The screw was apparently loose. Why? The assembler at the factory did not tighten it fully. Some might stop there and identify the worker for not doing his/her job properly. However, upon further investigation, one might determine that the design was

faulty not allowing the worker to completely perform the task of tightening the screw sufficiently. But why was the design not up to par? Perhaps the CAD (computer-aided design) tool that the designer used did not provide the designer with the correct information. As you can see, the root cause may have occurred long before your trim piece fell off. The intent of this sort of analysis isn't to fix the existing problem – your trim already failed. It is to prevent the same event from recurring on other products.

Another technique is called the "Five Whys." This can be thought of as constructing the primary path of the Root Cause Tree. The following example illustrates this: You were late. Why? Because you got lost. Why? You did not have directions...because you had to leave in a hurry....because you got home late....bad day at the office.... You can see that the *Five* is not the exact number of *Whys* to ask. Nor does this technique address what to do when there are multiple causes. Still, it is a powerful tool.

SWOT Analysis stands for Strengths, Weaknesses, Opportunities, and Threats Analysis. It is another specialized, and very useful, type of analysis. It is often used on business situations to plan strategy. The business identifies its internal strengths and weaknesses and any external opportunities and threats. It then becomes easier for planners to determine a course of action that plays to the strengths and opportunities while avoiding or eliminating the weaknesses and threats. This relatively simple process could be applied just as easily to an individual's situation. What are your strengths and weaknesses? What opportunities do you have; what threats do you face?

Financial Analysis is another critical tool that you have at your disposal. It does not have to be done with a spreadsheet. Indeed, technology can often be a barrier to obtaining the insights you need. Start by considering what it is that you need to understand. How many different numbers will have to be included? Start by making categories that have to be quantified. You can use the seven analysis questions to help you define them. The time spent outlining before doing any financial analysis will be well worth the effort.

Consider whether the numbers have a *time* attached to them. Will there be an hour or a decade's worth? Are there lots of details that need adding? Do individual numbers come from formulas? Do you understand these? Do you have all the numbers needed? Are you assuming some of them? Write down which. Can you create estimates for some of the numbers where you do not have hard data? You might try the analysis with a big version, a small one, and one in the middle. Make sure that the numbers make sense. Break an *annual* into a *monthly* if that helps you get a better grasp.

Financial analysis can be accomplished by comparing results: which is the smallest, the largest, the fastest changing, etc. You can graph your numbers in a dozen ways. This can make a result jump out to your eyes. Don't assume that your first answer is right. Edit the numbers; move each around; add more. Results should be understood – even if the answer is something like: "it will be between x & y, assuming that …; but if…then…"

Conclusion

In doing the work of analysis, there are a number of pitfalls to avoid. Probably the most important is to avoid erroneous assumptions. Of course, everyone makes assumptions all the time. The trick is to carefully consider the ones that you make and assure that they are valid.

Don't mistake activity for progress. Be aware that the point of your effort is to come closer to the truth – to increase your understanding. If you find that you are growing more and more confused, pause and back off from all the details. Sometimes they hide. There is great truth in the proverb: "You can't see the forest for the trees."

We have described breaking the situation into its components with our seven analysis questions used as the tools. Beware asking questions that you already know the answers to. You may be missing asking the more important questions – about things you don't know. Experts can help with this as can questions developed from other similar analyses.

Do not make the blunder in assuming that human behavior is always logical and completely open to your understanding. There are never engineering-like certainties where people are concerned.

Even a blind squirrel finds a nut every now and then. But doing analyses can help shine light into darkness. It helps point out the path allowing you to avoid pitfalls. It illustrates which are the treasures and which are not.

Chapter 9 – PLAN BETTER

Some people plan very well. Pleasing results are often seen quickly. Sometimes, however, results take years, if not decades, before it becomes apparent that "it just did not happen by accident."

Of those who do not plan well, perhaps the less said the better, but there will always be whispers: "What were they thinking?" followed by their own assessment: "We weren't." Whichever of the above categories is yours, be assured that you can learn to plan better.

Good planning is a critical step to achieving success. General and later President Dwight D. Eisenhower summed it up succinctly: "Plans are worthless. Planning is essential." He is echoed by Benjamin Franklin: "By failing to prepare, you are preparing to fail," adding that: "The Constitution only gives people the right to pursue happiness. You have to catch it yourself."

Luck in life helps – this cannot be denied – but it is not the way to success. Good planners share a number of disciplines, habits, and even tricks. They end up answering a number of important questions, even if they do not do so formally or are even aware of them.

The First Question

You might think that the first question is "How do I get *there* from *here*?" – but you'd be wrong. If you began that way, you'd be getting ahead of yourself. You might be creating something that is ineffective, if not altogether useless. This happens all the time, even to the experts. As much as you want to start asking about all the *steps* – you know, the things that seem so logical, each increasing the level of detail – please resist the urge. Don't ask: "What is the first step, the second…"

Instead, please, Please, PLEASE, start by asking the most critical question: "Where is *there*?" Albert Einstein is said to have remarked that if he had just one hour to save the world, he would spend fifty-five minutes defining the problem, and only five minutes finding the solution. This is another way of stressing the importance of defining *where is there*. This can also be written as: Make sure you know the problem you are trying to solve! The clearer you are about your destination, the better the chance you will reach it.

It is the executive's job to ask: "What are the business benefits?" This is a *where.* The reward of getting it right might be company survival. Firms that succeed, develop new products and enter markets as they cut costs and seek competitive advantage. The world is full of many Darwinistic forces – eat or be eaten. People and companies both deal with limited resources and conflicting demands.

Many things can be done to improve your definition of *there*. Write it down. The words you use set a tone, so be careful. Try to do a positive thing rather than avoiding a negative. Presuppose there are several good answers. Let others see what you come up with – their insight can be of great value. Break the problem down into its pieces. Look at the situation from *30,000 feet* to put it into perspective. It might be a part of a larger whole. Try to find the opposite; instead of thinking of ways to succeed, try determining the ways there are to fail. This will clarify both the pieces of the problem, and which of them are important. There are lots of tricks. Find your own, too.

Is there a special case with no clear *there*? At times, the journey itself is the goal (some say this about life itself). Consider a ramble through the autumn woods to encounter the unexpected, or letting the day pass as it will. Even these can be improved with a little foresight. Did you prepare lunch? If the goal is the search for the unexpected, having lunch with you might be better than being hungry in the woods.

What about when the thought is, "anywhere, better than here!" Even then, a little fore-thought helps. Moving toward something is better than lurching randomly about, whether you want to go away on vacation and don't know where to go; to move to a new home "away from here"; or to make a few changes but don't know what they might be.

In all of these cases, planning techniques will provide insight. Create a *where are we now* report – a status. It gives information about your destination and some of the factors involved: geography, money, time, whatever. These *considerations* help create alternatives and later, the answer to the question of destination.

Three Words

Planning begins with the *where*. But then what? There are tools that have come to epitomize the discipline of planning. Perhaps the most famous are the charts which give a visual representation of tasks with their order and dependencies. PERT charts were first used to run the U.S. Navy's Polaris missile program. But here is a great secret. *Planning is not about tools!*

Planning is just three words: *Reality*, *People*, and *Progress*.

✓ **Reality** means that dreams are not plans, nor is wishing and hoping. Plans are not glamorous; they are compilations of the ordinary. They include resources with their strengths and limitations, issues, risks, alternatives, and assumptions. Reality includes all of the laws of the Universe from physics to sociology and from economics to government. To ignore Reality is to beg to fail.

✓ **People** identifies the *who* are involved, affected, and even nearby. They are those who were, are, and will be the winners and losers; those who: do, are in charge, and need to know. People are also the unexpected. They do not act according to immutable laws – despite some psychologists'

assertions otherwise. They act in their own interest – or equally, in others' interest – seemingly randomly.

✓ **Progress** is the one thing all plans try to achieve. You want to move forward toward the goal(s). All the *what-next-steps* of your plan are there to move toward your *there*. Progress can be measured, imagined, lied about and, if things go right (and sometimes even if they go wrong), achieved.

Let's examine each of these three.   This is the foundation to layer other information upon as you get it. This will immediately improve your planning skills and allow them to continue to grow and bloom.

Reality begins with looking at those things you have available to work with on your journey forward. These include what is at hand and tangible like tools, raw materials, facilities, computers, etc. Things you cannot touch but are equally real are the amount of money available or the amount of credit you have. Time is another thing which is always to be considered.

All these things are your resources. They have strengths and limitations to be recognized and accounted for. What are you going to do with what you have? There are issues and challenges. Write them down along with what you are going to do about them. Can you live with them, fix them, or lessen their impact? You always have choices.

There are undesired things which may happen. Risks should be considered, but not all need a just-in-case plan.

The decision to create a *what-if scenario* is based on: its potential for devastating your work; its likelihood; and the time and energy you have available. Preparing will make you flexible and able to successfully respond to reality hitting you in the face – as it often does.

Assumptions made blindly have the potential to trip you up – and there are so many of them. Are you sure of everything that you will be depending on? Will they be available when you need them? Will an unexpected price increase blow up your budget? Will an expert really be one? Does one size fit all? Will the tunnel be wide enough; the bridge high enough; the river deep enough? When assumptions fail, there can be pain or laughter, glorious failure or even innovative solutions which bring success.

When the Hubble Space Telescope was launched by NASA in 1990, hopes were high that this incredible instrument would advance science by leaps and bounds. But it was soon seen that its images were out of focus. An investigation

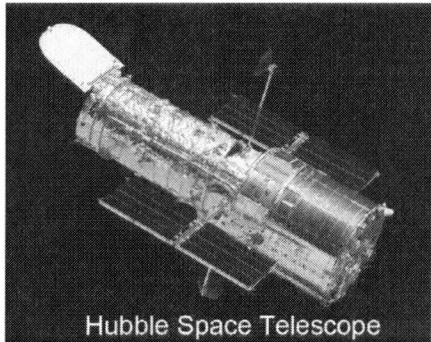

Hubble Space Telescope

found the mirror's maker, Perkin-Elmer, used an incorrectly calibrated tool to measure the mirror's shape. It reported the mirror was perfect. Two other tools did show that the mirror was flawed, but the company ignored this data! They assumed that the first tool was correct because it was newer. Later, in space, a costly Shuttle mission repaired the flawed telescope by giving it eyeglasses.

Russia's great city of St. Petersburg is known as the "city built on bones." Its construction on a vast swamp cost the lives of an enormous number of men; but provided us with one of history's great mistakes. Legend has it that the Czar's pencil accidentally hit his thumb as he drew the route of the link to Moscow. Today this *thumbprint* is immortalized in asphalt.

There is always a need for *reality*. Starting with it, you can add detail about what is needed, things to do, and possible solutions. Having a clear roadmap, that has been reviewed and verified, is a significant achievement.

The second law of Thermodynamics is *chaos tends to increase*. Organizational chaos may be seen in masses of directionless, meticulous work or endless contradictory efforts which then spawn more wasted effort. The first rail link across the United States almost did not happen – the east-west and west-east lines kept building past each other. Each line's construction crews continued laying tracks because each company got paid only as long as they continued to build.

When things get complicated as they usually do, things get harder. Important things are lost, hidden or get forgotten. This includes priorities. Some of the complexity involves choice between: what is critical and merely desirable; short or long-term goals; integrated or stand-alone solutions; and what is to be automated or kept manual. The list of choices can go on and on.

Planning is the discipline to deal with this. The *where* is always the first step; but both it and everything else must be *Reality-based,* meaning that they follow the laws of the Universe. The statement: "... a miracle happens now," does not build confidence nor is it a secret recipe for success. Don't use or depend on it! Another way to check on *reality* is to ask: "Does it pass the smell test?" Everything in the plan and its solution needs to be achievable and reasonable, including: what goes in and comes out, the way it works, the information, costs, legality, and all the rest. If you think anything stinks, it very well may. Check it out.

How is planning done where there are massive time pressures – when a situation explodes? Start with deciding on *there*. Prioritize. List what is available, and decide what should be done first. Are there plans already developed? Were there similar situations that can be learned from, utilized, or adapted? Pick a direction. Set a goal. The first, tentative step can be evaluated. Leaders often say "go in that direction," with the intention that they will adjust their path as they move. They recognize reality, not just that they can give orders.

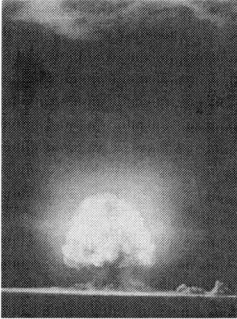

People, are all those who are involved, affected, and concerned; the "who does what to whom" and the "who is in charge." Identifying everyone is important, but this is only a first step. For each, learn, know, and provide for their needs, availability, reactions, etc.

How do you get people to do what you need? They can be channeled, taught, pushed, or they can agree with you. Even if the latter, do they have time to participate? Are they energetically committed, or just go through the motions? The people-part of plans for those actively involved is enormously important. Be clear. Communicate expectations, rewards, and punishments. When asking someone to do something, there are many considerations. What do you expect them to do? Are they working alone, or as a team? Do they depend on something else? When should it be finished; how good must it be?

It is always interesting to consider exactly how something should be done. But providing this in great detail to a subordinate is a sure way to kill innovation. In the end, when successful, make sure to congratulate them. Never skimp on praise or fail to recognize someone who has contributed. This is not flattery, but praise, and it will get you everywhere! If someone is not successful, don't be mad; simply work with them on a solution that will satisfy your needs. But make sure that they are aware of your displeasure.

In between the start and the finish, there is the critical *doing*, during which the plan is used as a guide, to coordinate, and is updated as reality changes. People are

U.S. Capital Building

the critical element of the doing stage. It is not about the plan.

The *who-needs- to-know* is part of the plan, too. You may have considered those affected and nearby but there are many others who fall into this category. Does what is going to be done interest the Federal, State, or Local government? Does money need to be acquired, returned, or controlled – and by whom? Who wins and loses; what about producers, consumers, and competitors?

Everyone needs to get what they need to perform: tools, information, or help. Start with making sure they get clear, understandable, and efficient communications.

People need to know! Their proper care and feeding is essential.

Plan to communicate. This can be from the top of a pyramid down, or information can flow out from the center of a wheel. You may choose to allow anyone to reach everyone else. There are old and new methods available starting with just talking face-to-face. There is the phone, speeches, and now, e-mail, texts, Twitter, wikis, forums, videos, and many other new-technologies. Each of these styles can work, but you can't take that for granted. Use several. Pay attention to what is working and then try harder.

There is no difference for a business. The executives need to be connected to the company. Projects are monitored and resources shifted as the situation or priorities change. Everyone must be in the loop and leveraging their vast pool of knowledge effectively. As the artist paints a mural, so the executive develops the big picture into which details can be fit. As a conductor orchestrates harmony out of discord the manager seeks to deliver success in the face of competition, contradiction, and chaos.

Engineering and Art are often thought of as the antithesis of each other, yet both should be found in a successful plan. There is, however, an almost visceral abhorrence of *Art* in the hard business world. This is acknowledged, backhandedly, by titles such as *The Art of the Deal* and *Art of War*. Non-engineering, non-technical skills are seen almost as black art, i.e. magic. This is also true when setting direction and gaining consensus. This is not easy to get right.

Progress is the reason that you plan. It describes how to move forward toward your goal(s). This means that it now is time to ask all the *what next* questions to identify the steps to move you toward your *there*.

As you know by now, you always have choices and they should be explicitly included in your plan. Are you going big or small; fast or slow; being innovative or safe? Will *low-hanging fruit* be gathered first or will the important things be done first? The list of choices is endless; it is the act of planning which allows for their consideration.

This analysis of your choices can be very hard work. These choices may involve creating multiple plans as you consider the alternatives: cost, time, and risk. Some engineering firms preach *fit-for-purpose* as the criteria for when to stop engineering something toward perfection. This is a brief phrase to remind you to keep in mind all of the economic, technological, and business-based considerations so your efforts won't continue forever. Recognize when *enough is enough*. There is a point beyond which your efforts will achieve diminishing returns and add no additional value.

Apollo 13
Service Module Damage

Of all the considerations you will make in the development of your plan, the above-mentioned *smell test* is the funniest but perhaps the most important. Let's put this another way: there are *atta-boys* and *whoopses*. Some experts estimate that the benefit from one hundred (100) of the former equals the loss from one (1) of the latter (the cost of one *whoops* is often much higher than that). Your plan never wants to encounter a *whoops*! One small mistake made in a factory caused the aborting of the Apollo 13 mission in 1970, and nearly cost the lives of three astronauts – Whoops!

Your plan's steps are typically sequential but doing things in parallel can speed them up. The question, always, is whether the benefits from the added complexity of doing things in parallel will be worth it, i.e. will you get any *bang for your buck*. Sometimes doing so, works. Other-times you can find yourself amidst a chaos of your own making.

Be sure to identify which step must come before another. The chain of these is called the critical path which defines the absolute minimum amount of time a plan can take. The duration of work is defined by the critical path.

By itself, a plan is not real. It is an idea, a progression which might take place. When you read about a successful plan, what is meant is that not only was a direction set, but the path was actually trod, and its end reached. A great plan, poorly executed, will not a success make.

There are lots of things that are critical parts of execution, and the most important is often communication, which we are here emphasizing again. This is letting your left hand know what your right is doing, or more generally, getting the various members of the effort to coordinate. Make sure that each knows where in the mosaic their part fits.

Other critical elements include having the knowledge required to perform a task. The resources needed for any step must be there when needed. Manufacturers often try to save money by not keeping an inventory, insisting their suppliers deliver parts just before they are installed, the so-called *just-in-time inventory* system. You might need to get approvals or permits and Government ones are notoriously difficult to obtain – not to mention time-wasting.

One last thing: plans should never be *set in stone*. There is a famous military axiom regarding planning attributed to several great minds: "No plan survives first contact with the enemy." Be prepared to revise your plans while they are in motion to accommodate new information, experience, an unexpected event, or even a mistake (they happen).

Conclusion

Planning is hard. Life is complex. What you don't know is infinite; what you don't control, enormous.

You have choices. You can lie down and get run over, fight chaotically, or try to see how you might deal with what is happening – and perhaps gain an advantage in the struggle.

This third option might be best. It is not cheating. It might even be fun.

Chapter 10 – LEAD BETTER

This chapter is about another critical skill that you probably have not studied. This may be a result of the attitude implicit in the saying: "Leaders are born, not made," which conveys a sense that you either are, or you are not, a leader. This view does not help you. Successful leaders can have many different traits. Knowing what they are and using them can only help make you more successful.

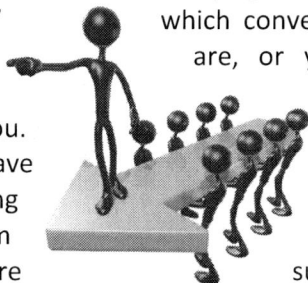

Consider the words of the Greek philosopher, Plato: "For a man to conquer himself is the first and noblest of all victories...but to be conquered by yourself is shameful and vile." You must know yourself before you can lead others.

But what is leadership? Is it getting others to do what you do not? That seems to be a terrible way of looking at the subject. A more positive view: To lead is to love something so deeply that others join you. Consider Mahatma Gandhi who seems to have considered both sides: "Leadership at one time meant muscles; but today it means getting along with people."

Does leadership imply a destination or a goal? Is the leader responsible for determining the timeframe and the plan? What about consideration of the future because short-term goals may conflict with long-term ones?

There are many sayings about leadership, e.g. "It is lonely at the top." Each of them may capture a small portion of what it takes – or not. There are many different facets of leadership, its styles, and theories of it. In the 1960's, MIT's Douglas McGregor proposed the Theory X or Y model of management and labor. In the *X* case, workers are considered lazy; in the *Y* Case, they are ambitious. Later, a whole host of other theories followed, including Theory Z. In short, there is no single, agreed-upon theory of leadership that covers all people and situations.

The Few, the Proud

We can, however, agree that there are places where the need for leadership is recognized and where those aspiring to lead receive training. These include the various U.S. military academies, from the Air Force to the Marines; the latter of which lists 14 Leadership Traits used for their officers' training. These have been put into an acronym: *JJ DID TIE BUCKLE*. We present them here as an excellent description of what traits a leader should possess:

- ✓ *Justice:* Giving reward and punishment according to the merits of the case in question. The ability to administer a system of rewards and punishments impartially and consistently.
- ✓ *Judgment*: The ability to weigh facts and possible courses of action in order to make sound decisions.
- ✓ *Dependability*: The certainty of proper performance of duty.
- ✓ *Initiative*: Taking action in the absence of orders.
- ✓ *Decisiveness*: Ability to make decisions promptly and to announce them in a clear, forceful manner.

✓ **Tact**: The ability to deal with others without creating hostility.

✓ **Integrity**: Uprightness of character and soundness of moral principles.

✓ **Enthusiasm**: The display of sincere interest and exuberance in the performance of duty.

✓ **Bearing**: Creating a favorable impression in carriage, appearance, and personal conduct always.

✓ **Unselfishness:** Avoidance of providing for one's own comfort and personal advancement at the expense of others.

✓ **Courage:** A mental quality that recognizes fear of danger or criticism, but enables a Marine to proceed in the face of it with calmness and firmness.

✓ **Knowledge:** Understanding of a science or an art. The range of one's information, including professional knowledge and an understanding of your Marines.

✓ **Loyalty:** The quality of faithfulness to Country, the Corps, and unit, and to one's seniors, subordinates, and peers.

✓ **Endurance:** The mental and physical stamina measured by the ability to withstand pain, fatigue, stress, and hardship.

Other phrases have been used to describe leadership and it is interesting to see how very many of them are subsumed by the Marines' list. These include: inspiring, having passion, ego-submergence, risk-taking and taking responsibility. Some of these descriptions are prosaic, others eloquent. Some are beautiful: being willing to stand out in a crowd; having an open mind and an open heart; or (a favorite) to inspire others to contribute to a dream.

Tricks

Courage: There are a huge number of things that can be done by a leader to help his cause. Are they tricks or simply the product of a mind trying to help others? Consider one of them, given to us by Plato, on a Marine-Corp trait: "Courage is knowing what not to fear."

Decisiveness: Get started toward accomplishing your task, but remember that if you don't know where you are going, any road will take you there – so get started in the right direction and refine as you move forward.

Motivation: One factory manager asked the day crew how many they produced in a shift. He then took a piece of chalk and wrote the number as large as he could on a wall. The night crew saw the number, asked what it was, and proceeded to exceed it. For each of several shifts the number increased. The manager was pleased and showed it. He increased everyone's wages because the increased output directly contributed to the company's increased profits.

Dr. Martin Luther King Jr. Delivering His "I Have a Dream" Speech

Knowledge: Ideally, when you lead, you are an expert on the topic at hand. However, realistically, there will probably be others who are working with you who know more. The goal is not to be an expert, but to be well-versed on the subject. Know the language used – the key words and phrases. Know some facts and figures

– do research. Be able to speak intelligently on the subject.

Tact: You must always be compassionate and understanding of others. You are an authority, not an autocrat or a bureaucrat. Listen to others' opinions; weigh the facts. Temper your decision by taking into account how others will react versus the needs of the task at hand. When you make a decision, be clear and decisive but not argumentative or condescending. Reading this, it is clear that the image of a screaming manager is far away. Can they be successful? Can they be more successful?

This list of *tricks* could go on and on. Feel free to add to it yourself. There is one additional *trick* to consider – one that is implied in the *JJ DID TIE BUCKLE* list. Consider the need for political skills. Politics is very much in the media, seeming more and more prevalent as the years pass. But the word *politician* seems to be in disrepute – and possibly even worse in that they always seem to be lawyers!

But political skills do matter. So what are those skills? Is it as simple as the skill of getting along with people? Are the skills related to the identification and achievement of common interests? Leaders must often involve themselves in politics – either informally or formally. It is an important skill which is difficult for a leader to delegate. They are not covered here beyond a simple example that underlies the reality of the ugliness of politics. Consider the case where a two-thirds majority is needed out of three votes with two opposed to each other. The remaining one has *power*, because his/her vote is the deciding one. A simple quote, variously attributed, warns: "Laws are like sausages; it is best not to see them being made."

Great Leaders

There are numerous examples of leadership to draw from. Here are a very few that illustrate how leadership can span a wide spectrum: religious and military; male and female; modern and historical; government and private. For each, their own words show their philosophy and how it was put into practical action. Can you recognize the leadership traits that each leader embodies best?

Pope John Paul II was the absolute monarch of the world's smallest nation, Vatican City. Years before his pontification, the Pope was famously derided by Joseph Stalin: "How many [army] divisions has the Pope?" The small size of the Holy See (another name for the Vatican) does not inspire; it is the size of a small golf course, just a fifth of a square mile. There are no street addresses in the country nor are there any permanent citizens.

Karol Józef Wojtyła was called to the priesthood after Poland had been overrun by the Nazis. He was forced to study in secret while working in a quarry to avoid deportation. After his ordination, his flock was suppressed by a Communist government which denied God. John Paul II became the first non-Italian to sit in the chair of Peter in over 400 years. His reign was one of the longest in history, following one of the shortest – John Paul I died after only 33 days as pontiff. Karol's great moral courage helped him bear his many burdens which included getting shot during an assassination attempt in 1981.

Yet the Holy Father's belief that "Freedom consists not in doing what we like, but in having the right to do what we ought," is seen in his answer to Stalin's question. Pope John Paul II returned to Poland to celebrate an outdoor mass attended by hundreds of thousands. This proved to be a major blow to the legitimacy of the Regime. Soon, not only did Communism fall in Poland, but also across the entire Eastern Block and even the Soviet Union itself.

The someday-to-be Saint John Paul II reached out with great moral clarity to all: youth, other religions, and many cultures in his writings, personal appearances, and travels. He did not command armies; he just showed them, as he would have said it, "His way."

What was it about *this* Pope that made him so widely loved and respected by Catholics and non-Catholics alike? His position as pontiff gave him the authority and ability to take the world stage, this is true. But many others hold and have held that position but have not made a similar impact. Whether you ascribe to his teachings or not, it is clear that it was his leadership that was the key. His clear, consistent direction, his moral courage to stand up for his beliefs in a world which looks the other way, and his initiative in taking his message directly to the masses are what made him the powerful and impactful leader that he was.

*   *   *   *   *

Ulysses S. Grant was working as a clerk in his father's leather store when the Civil War began. Seven years later, he was elected the eighteenth President of the

United States. This unprecedented rise was a direct consequence of the faithful and successful pursuit of his very simple life's philosophy: "Everyone has his superstitions. One of mine has always been when I started to go anywhere... never to turn back or stop until... [I get there]."

This was true of all his campaigns including the capture of Vicksburg. The most famous of all of them, however, was against General Lee. It lasted over a year, with his determination clear: "I propose to fight it out on this line if it takes all summer." It ended at Appomattox, with the surrender of the great Army of Northern Virginia.

His last campaign was not as dramatic; but was typical of the man. After leaving the Presidency, he was doubly stricken, losing his fortune to fraud and being afflicted by throat cancer. He responded by setting a goal and achieving it, despite great obstacles. The two-volume *Personal Memoirs of Ulysses S. Grant*, published by Mark Twain, is ranked among the greatest works of literature in American history. Hand-written, though almost debilitated by pain at the end, Grant finished only days before succumbing to his greatest and final foe.

President Grant has been maligned. Called a "drunkard" by some, he instead only suffered from intense migraine headaches. Labeled a "butcher" by others, Lee's losses in battle were greater. The question:

"Who is buried in Grant's Tomb?" is symbolic of historical disregard. It is fitting that everyone leans over a railing to see his sarcophagus. They are bowing to this humble leader of the first million-soldier army in history. He presided over the reconstruction of a South that he graciously and generously treated after forcing them to *unconditionally surrender*.

Despite advantages in the number of men and the amount of resources available to the Union army before General Grant assumed command, it was poorly led – one might argue there was no leadership at all. Grant's endurance, knowledge, and initiative ultimately created a successful fighting force. His personal courage brought him through the many adversities that he faced as a general, a president, and as a person.

*   *   *   *   *

Before Jack Welch was born, President Calvin Coolidge captured what many believe to be an important aspect of the Nation's uniqueness: "The business of America is business." Of the many captains of industry who have crossed the industrial stage, Welch's philosophy might be the easiest to understand: "The team with the best players wins."

GE Building NYC

Jack's career at General Electric almost ended after a single year. He was frustrated at the vast bureaucracy that had sprouted since Thomas Edison founded the company. He resigned, but was induced to return. Welch stressed clarity of mission: to be first or second in a market – or out entirely. He rewarded success generously but pruned ruthlessly, firing the bottom 10% of GE's managers each year. As part of his seeking efficiencies, he reduced GE's employment by a quarter, eliminating over 100,000 people in a 5-year period.

He became the youngest-ever CEO of GE, its longest serving, and the most successful. Under his tenure, he raised the worth of the company from 14 to over $410 billion, making it the most valuable company in the world at the time. Many of his tenets and practices have been copied by firms around the world, prompting *Forbes Magazine*, in 1999, to declare him to be the "Manager of the Century." Certainly, his leadership mattered to many.

Welch's leadership was founded on his clarity and consistency of mission. He was unwavering and unambiguous about his plans and business beliefs. One could argue that his practices were ruthless but the results are hard to dispute. His purpose was obviously driven toward the greater good.

*   *   *   *   *

Vince Lombardi, like all the other football coaches, led an army of only a few dozen men into *battle*; but unlike most teams, his consistently won. His success was such that the Super Bowl trophy is named in his honor. But, while his most famous quote is: "Winning isn't everything, it is the only thing," this hides the critical elements responsible for his teams' successes.

The challenge for all leaders is to get their team to willingly pay the price needed to succeed. In this he excelled. Recordings of his motivational speeches are still being used in many fields. Some of his philosophical attributes apply to other endeavors. Coach Lombardi did not just believe in discipline, hard work, and teamwork, he brought these concepts to every practice where they were made real. His practices were known for their relentless pursuit of perfection. His was the world of football, so he was not an idealist, instead understanding "Perfection is not attainable, but if we chase perfection we can catch excellence."

Yet for all the success his teams had, when attempting to determine his secret to success, consider this: he put perseverance ahead of all others: "The greatest accomplishment is not in never falling, but in rising again after you fall." Sadly, he was stricken by cancer, dying weeks after its diagnosis.

This coach's hallmarks as a leader are motivation and endurance. For his accomplishments, but perhaps more for how he made them, he is immortalized in that trophy coveted by so many.

*   *   *   *   *

General George Patton led armies to victory in the Second World War. He was considered to be the Allies' greatest general by their opponents. The Germans almost disregarded the Normandy invasion because Patton was poised as a feint elsewhere – at Calais. He was outspoken to a fault – remembered for his inopportune comments, eccentric style, and, most egregiously, thinking a hospitalized soldier malingering and calling him a coward before slapping him.

His success may have had much to do with technology; he was the first U.S. Officer to be assigned to the newly-formed U.S. Tank Corps in WWI. During his European campaigns, he was a master of the coordination of his armored units with tactical air support, allowing his armies to move rapidly on a narrow salient, while protecting his flanks from counterattack by aerial observation. His Third Army was legendary, yet its greatest feat may have been a logistic operation conducted during the Battle of the Bulge – disengaging from one hot battle to turn to another, distant one.

Besides tactical brilliance, his thinking was also strategic. He was one of the first, upon the defeat of the Germans, to argue that the Soviets were the greater threat. He wanted the German Army rebuilt as an ally to help free Eastern and Central Europe from Soviet domination.

But deeper than his war-systems understanding was an obsession at the human level. He made himself act as a leader sans self-doubt, believing that attitude honored his men and would motivate them. He adopted a distinctive persona as a leader and professional soldier – polished helmet, boots, and ivory-handled pistols – to further motivate his subordinates. He offered his men: "Better to fight for something than live for nothing," adding of his expectations: "Don't tell people how to do things, tell them what to do and let them surprise you with their results." At war's end, he was in a seemingly minor automobile accident, breaking his neck, and ending his life. He is buried at the head of the troops he led.

This General understood leadership; his actions and statements were all intended to inspire his troops. A controversial figure for his unbridled tongue and sometimes-arcane beliefs, his success on the battlefield is legendary. His subordinates rewrote the book on armor tactics and would apparently do the impossible for him – perhaps because they were more afraid of him than the enemy. Decisiveness, initiative, consistency, bearing, knowledge, courage and endurance all graced this leader.

*   *   *   *   *

Mother Teresa stands at the opposite end of the spectrum occupied by Generals, Captains of Industry, Super Bowl winning coaches, and even a Catholic Pope.

She was born Agnes Gonxha Bojaxhiu in Skopje, Yugoslavia, a physically small woman. Her Lord's call led to the Loreto Sisters of Ireland, a Catholic order of nuns whose missionaries educate young girls. She was sent to India, took the name Teresa with her vows, and spent 15 years teaching at St. Mary's School for Girls in Calcutta.

Her axiom "Be faithful in small things because it is in them that your strength lies," is a *little* philosophic

principle. It is similar to another of hers: "Love begins by taking care of the closest ones." Mother Teresa chose to do this for the poorest of the poor, the people who no one wanted, those who no one loved. She petitioned the Church for permission to begin working in the vast slums by herself. She began by teaching, ministering to those dying from terrible diseases and to those living literally on the street.

Her labors were amplified by volunteers who joined her. The first was one of her former students. In two years, there were thirteen in her band and it was officially recognized by the diocese. They opened facilities. An abandoned temple became a home for those dying from Hansen's disease – Leprosy – and also for unwanted children.

Her labors resulted in world-wide media coverage and a plethora of awards including the Nobel Prize. Upon her death, the Catholic Church declared her a Saint. The movement she founded and led until her death, the Missionaries of Charity has spread across the world with thousands of members. All this, from a small woman deemed *ordinary* by one of her fellow novices in Ireland.

Her leadership began with not just her deep feelings, but her loving; it was continued by her personal involvement. Mother Teresa cared so much for her mission that she never paid any attention to anything written in her praise; she never bothered to correct an incorrect date of birth written in the many articles and books in her honor. It was not about her. Rather, her mission was to show the love of God to those unloved. For many, she succeeded. Clearly, unselfishness and endurance are hers.

Conclusion

Please, investigate the lives of more of the very many who are not included here. Expand the list of *tricks*, *techniques* and *political skills*. In doing so, you might find confirmation of what you have just read or additional insight into leadership which has not been provided. Most of all, you might find a sense of amazement of all that they accomplished in the face of enormous adversity.

Throughout these examples, you can see many of the Marines' leadership qualities reflected. The leaders highlighted here had to overcome huge adversity and made significant impacts on the human condition. Yours is not necessarily as significant – except that yours is critically important to you. You may not need to lead an army or be CEO of a major corporation. You can take these qualities and weave them into your persona; apply them to your situation. With a little forbearance, you can lead as well.

There is no reason that you cannot learn, apply, and garner the fruits of their labors.

~KNOWLEDGE SECTION~

Chapter 11 – FRIENDS, INTERRUPTED

This chapter will provide a sense of where everything comes from – and this really does mean everything! The information is science-based and not the simple "from God" answer that was given me long ago in my Grammar School. But, and this is a BIG but, you may see how science and Saint Agatha's intersect in a few pages. I hope you will find it interesting to get this information from a true story.

Friends

What do you mean that you don't know where your house was? You lived there for 16 years!"

Joe and Irene turned from the mass of tangled brambles that filled what had once been their yard and looked at each other.

"Well, Mike" Irene drawled, we haven't been back to the old homestead for, what-say Joe, a dozen years more or less. It was some time 'fore that, the house got burned down. Everything is just grown over now."

Joe, and his sister Irene, were my best friends on the mountain. Babcia Helen had moved up there after Jadgi died. Each summer growing up, Mama and Tata sent me to her. My escape began days after school ended, with the hot and dirty city streets receding through the rear window of our Chrysler. But it was not until many years later that I understood my parents' wisdom. Those were the summers of the inner-city riots. Watts and Newark are today memories, but my family owned a neighborhood bar – and it must have been quite a target, despite the baseball bat Tata kept beneath the long, mahogany bar.

Even so, for them, the biggest reason for me to go was to help my Grandmother. Why me of all the grandchildren? Who knows? Perhaps I was just the one who needed discipline the most. But it is clear now that I was blessed; the mountain was a magical place for a young boy – a private universe – far removed from the city. It was an interruption in the urban rhythm of my young life; regretfully, one which will not come again.

I'd joke that Babcia was cruel, but the world has changed and you might misunderstand. Up there, play followed chores, and there were a lot of them. She made me clean my room, help take care of the yard, and even wield a hatchet to cut wood for the stove. Doing these things for someone you love and who adores you even more was not work, but rather a promotion within my family. I was able to act as a young man before my years had earned that appellation. It was wonderful.

…and so was the play. The terraced yards were acres in size – hers almost five – huge fields for imagination to run wild and free. We never wandered far, and in the heat of the summer, games of Monopoly on shady porches overlooking the banks could continue for days. They were interrupted by lemonade, raspberry picking, or just lying on the grass looking at the clouds. Lacking iPods, TVs, or the Web, we were too young, and too full of life, to be bored.

"You want to go up and take a look at the tunnel before we leave?" the adult me asked them on the day I'd returned after so long.

"Never been there," Joe allowed, much to my surprise. "Mama let on that she used to walk through it to the Bear Valley for blueberries, but that was years and years ago, back when she was a young girl."

Colliery Road led up from the town to the patch of homes on the side of the mountain. It skirted the black proof that coal had been dug nearby. Townies called it the "burning banks" – a coal mine's black vomit. The enormous pile had been created through the efforts of hundreds of children, cleaning the coal year-round, for almost one hundred years. Theirs was a life of sweat all the summer, cold in the winter, and always the choke of ore-dust. But beneath the bank was a – literally – hot secret. The coal refuse pile was on fire – underground. It burned for decades. When we were children, deep cracks in the ground marked the hot spots; glowing blue at night; rain turning their smokes into steam.

We were luckier than we knew, though. One town's deep fire had forced its evacuation. No one lives in Centralia anymore. Another valley suffered a far worse tragedy. The small South-Wales village of Aberfan suffered agonies after its waste pile slid down their mountain during a rainstorm. This black avalanche buried their school. It took only seconds on that terrible day for one-hundred-sixteen children and twenty-eight adults to die.

A hundred years before that, when our mine was in full operation, the Philadelphia elite grew wealthy from their shares of the miners' hard work and long hours. But unions were not yet born, so darkness, dirt, and danger paid little. Strong arms dug with pick and shovel; the only light there came from a candle, attached to the miner's helmet. Later, steam power and TNT were introduced but they just made it more dangerous. Many lives were lost by explosion, collapse, and perhaps most terrifyingly, by gas. In just one incident, this invisible phantasm felled over fifty men who'd hitched a ride on our ore train.

Though spare time was scant, the miners had family and a vast pride. They planted cabins, orchards, and gardens whose use spanned generations. The small homes were filled with noise: mothers and grandmothers caring for the many young; their maternal warmth supplemented by enamel cook-stoves in the back kitchen, and the parlor's fireplace. Beneath the floorboards was the root cellar, filled with all manner of staples: carrots, yams, and potatoes. But best of all, were the jars of home-made preserves. Cherry was my favorite.

Roads had not yet known automobiles, so everyone lived within walking distance of the mine's opening. No matter the season, fathers and sons watched the sunrise make long shadows as they trod the rough tracks uphill. The daylight hours were spent down the shaft, at the coal-face. The flickering light from their candles – later small lamps worn intimately – did not dispel the damp, chill air, so was small comfort. Electricity would not arrive for 70 years. Canaries and mules accompanied them below; the one serving as warning, the other as muscle.

Down the hill was the sorely needed company wash-house, hard used. In it was another of the mountain's gifts – tons of cold water from the hole. Again, the largess was not extended to the miners; their houses would always lack running water. The community's deep well was a fifteen minute walk for tired men and even longer for 10-year-old boys. The route followed the railroad past the last of the houses and down a narrow path through the woods. An irregular pool of blackness, fifty feet deep and roughly circular was bridged by a winch. Its chain was rusty with bucket dented from long use. The drawn water was poured into a carrying pail for the return trip. Walking at dusk caused many a misstep, and a spill would mean a revisit to the well.

They took their ease in the softness of the evening, sheltering on the porch in their rocking chairs. With boots off, they watched grass, vegetables, and children grow. The apple and cherry trees that sheltered the swings were out front, backdrop to the fireflies. Hidden behind was the outhouse. Later, its half-rubble-filled depths – an empty grave – would be the last sign that a family once lived nearby.

As the three of us stood in the late afternoon sun, we could hear the mountain's loneliness in the silence. A hundred years of history had ended with the mine's closing. Questions of what to pack – painful choices – detailed the sad exodus that began before we were born. One by one, families moved down into the valley, or beyond, over the pass. Tomorrow, a rich chapter will conclude with the passing of the last of yesterday's families.

But even as their backs receded, nature began its reclamation: invading the empty houses; creeping into dark bedrooms; and spreading dankly over the wood floors. Wild foliage reseeded the gardens, the irregular splashes of color memory of the old flower beds. Slowly the traces faded: paths hid, buildings shrank, and foundations buried – so that even those who had once lived there could no longer find their own front steps.

Forty years ago, I was too little to explore the mountain alone. Each year's autumn brought my Father to take me home. For the whole of that happy weekend, my lonely shadow would merge with his as we walked the mountain. With his strong arm across my shoulders, I would prattle on, telling him about my entire summer. With him protecting me, Babcia would let us explore. Together, we would go all the way up to the forbidden tunnel.

A Brief Interruption

The years had not been kind to the unpaved road. The rains had deepened and widened the forgotten wagon tracks. Cleansed of their protective layer of dirt, jagged stones emerged to grab and twist unwary ankles.

I was not worried about finding the tunnel. It was built for a steam locomotive, but the tracks were long gone. The opening was huge, framed by giant stone wings. Above it was a massive concrete lintel. The seasons had worn the deeply-inscribed dates almost unreadable, possibly "1868" and "1919." The aura of age was tangible, felt in the chilly, dank air emanating from its depths. A red-brick-lined arch extended inwards. Forcefully driven into the side of the mountain, it ended thirty feet on where a jumble of tumbled rock announced a long-ago cave-in. What lay beyond was a dark secret.

"If the tunnel went through the mountain, I wonder if it was built by the railroad your dad worked for," I asked.

"Do you know if there is another opening up here, or was this the mine?"

"Don't know for sure. I heard tell there's another opening down below, but that's a-ways from here." Joe paused. "Thinking on it, how did coal get here?"

We wanted answers, and so began an odyssey back through time and space seeking a truth that we were once too young to even imagine. But the world had changed in the many years since we'd last all been together. Nothing, it seems, is permanent.

A sea of information now confronted us; clues to deeper truths, but little in black and white. Shades of gray are everywhere – words and images that mislead. Who has ever seen the sun rise or set? It does neither. It is we who move, as the Earth spins on its axis. The idea of "forever & ever" is romantic, but is not reality; both time and space began with the *Big Bang*, the event that formed the universe. What happened before is a mystery. If the scientists are right, there was no *before*. God only knows what will follow – and those who deny His existence do not know.

At the instant of the Big Bang, the Universe was infinitely small and infinitely hot. In its impossibly small space was everything that is today – all matter and energy. Its perfect symmetry was evident in all directions. There was only that single point – a singularity of existence.

But its symmetry was not to last. Instantly, violently, and with more force than can be imagined, that singularity expanded. Within a few minutes, the first atoms

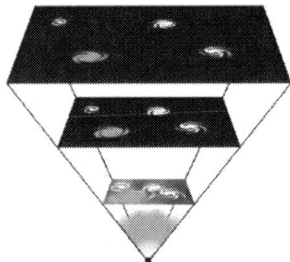

formed. Emerging from the chaos was a vast cloud of gas and dust. It coalesced; the clumps grew to enormous size and incredible pressures made them ignite. Order gradually emerged as the lesser bodies began to encircle the greater – flaming planets around flaring suns. Over the course of billions of years the planets slowly cooled until at least one crust would support life.

History is found beneath our feet and even in the sky. At night we marvel at the multitude of stars sliding across the heavens with the seasons. Telescopes reach out to distant galaxies to show stars' birth and death, alien planets, and possibly distant life. Everything began with that explosion, and the residue – the galaxies, our Milky Way among them – continues to flee through space. So the Earth never actually returns to where it began the year. Its orbital motion is augmented by the movement of our Sun within the Galaxy and the Galaxy through the Universe – all in an epic orchestration whose grand design is yet unclear. The Universe's expansion is actually accelerating; scientists debate whether it will always do so. The likely outcome, however, is that the Universe will continue to expand forever.

In fact, this expansion is not simply the movement of galaxies away from one another; it is the creation of added space between and among them. The space itself is expanding. This concept is hard to grasp but has consequences that impact the future of the entire Universe. It can be compared to the expansion of a bubble. If you had a polka-dot bubble – as strange as that sounds – each dot could represent a galaxy. As the bubble is enlarged, each of the dots moves away from the others. From the

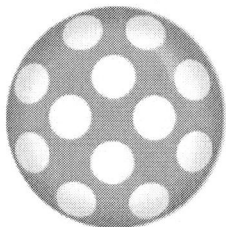

perspective of any one dot, all of the other dots are moving away as the surface of the bubble gets larger. No dot is at the center of the expansion in this two-dimensional projection. This is what is happening to our Universe except that it occurs in all three dimensions at once.

We stand far up the side of Big Lick Mountain, behind is its companion, Bear, across there is Berry. These mountains are framing the setting sun. In the night sky above, our naked eyes can sometimes see the gas giant, Jupiter. Science's progress amazes, but is often interrupted. Galileo's telescope thrust a far-seeing eye into the sky to discover its circling moons now collectively named in his honor – the *Galilean* moons: Io, Europa, Ganymede and Callisto. But the Catholic Church arrested him, declaring "only the Church knows what is," diminishing Italy's role in the advancement of science for hundreds of years.

Galilean Moons: Callisto Ganymede Europa Io

Jupiter was named after one of the Gods of the ancient world. Three thousand years have reduced that past's traces to mere bits and pieces. These are continually being erased by development. Being close and personal brings understanding, but distance yields perspective. So much was, and is no longer. More is unrecognized, despite overwhelming proofs – perhaps deliberately to avoid confronting the enormity of God's creation. How can the phrase "unmoving as a stone" be uttered when many huge boulders were placed by mile-high glaciers millennia past? Continents' slow drift across the molten core of

our planet is writ large on the map by the fit of Africa into South America. Other evidences abound: earthquakes; the explosive power of the volcano; and the stark majesty of Everest and K2 who, along with their Himalayan brothers, are being thrust ever-higher into the sky as India slowly slides under Tibet.

Four hundred thousand millennia past, vast primordial swamps lay athwart the equator. They rose only a few feet above the surface of the ocean, but sustained a riot of vegetation. The continents' movement stretched, compressed, and changed the contours of that world. Today, in places, the swamps have been driven thousands of feet below the surface; brought to the tops of mountains elsewhere. Their crushed remains were transformed by time, pressure, and heat to become the fuels of our world. Saudi Arabia floats atop a sea of oil; Pennsylvania rests on beds of coal. In that state's southeast corner, the edge of one ancient swamp was once seen clearly on the northern side of the valley that bears our town's name.

Friends, Resumed

My grandfather had been a miner – perhaps even here. I've no memories of him, just the one photograph taken of him standing beside my older brother. Jadgi's voice went silent before my pilgrimages began, so he can't share his story, though I'm now ready to listen. My son will hear less; the anecdotes shared over the dinner table are gradually fading. With each passing year, the echoes of the raucous cacophony that had filled the dining room diminish, through whispers, to silence.

Williamstown was once known as "the town with the best Anthracite coal," a name well earned from the "black gold" found nearby. The first settlers had found that the mountain had stripes, hidden beneath the virgin foliage. The largest was almost 20 feet thick. It is now gone, an erasure that took almost 100 years to accomplish. Today the last of those black bands is being reduced by never-tiring machines whose mechanical arms take the place of the thousands who once labored at this task. When they are finished, quiet will again return to the mountain. Over time, the collapsed tunnel mouth will slowly fill and knowledge of what lay beneath will be lost. There are always fewer of that generation left – a loss more costly than future generations' missing the short-cut to the high valley.

The stripes? Open your kitchen cabinet and stare at your plates, stacked high. Move closer and the edges grow huge just before your naked eye touches. Each of those stripes was the edge of a coal plate covering hundreds of square miles; a remnant of the vast swamps from the dawn of life. They traveled far to reach their resting places.

We grew up there, but it was clear that we neither understood what lay so close, nor knew to ask. Was I an outsider, resented because I had been sent to spend the summer with my grandmother? No, never. For all those summers, Joe and Irene were simply my *bestest* friends.

I'd lost touch with them for a lifetime, even forgetting their family name. Memories fade even as new ones are born. A chance association brought it all back and a call to information opened a door to a past when we were all younger. Their invitation to visit brought together adults who had never met – three whose lives had intertwined, parted, and reconnected once more. We discovered that our hidden childhood selves remained just beneath the mind's surface, not buried so deep that a long-ago friendship was forever gone.

That trip reunited friends who had each remained young – in the others' memory and in their hearts. The decades apart mattered not at all. The friendship, interrupted, continued – and is proof that some things don't change.

Conclusion

The dirt under your feet has a story. Our Earth has a story. Knowing where and how things started matters, but for many, it is news that somehow never arrived. This knowledge is not simply to make you sound more worldly or well-read at a dinner party, it adds to your tool kit of facts and, more importantly, to your perspective of your place in the Universe.

The moral of this little tale is very simple, that perspective can answer many questions. Our presentation of how the Universe was created has been presented as an *interruption* in the course of a true story. Perhaps you knew all the information in that section, and if you did, hopefully you enjoyed the story anyway.

Chapter 12 – EVERYDAY MIRACLES

You are surrounded by wonders every day. Some might even consider our Universe to be bursting with miracles – awesome processes and events that are within our grasp to comprehend and yet, beyond our imagining how they were created. There are many of these miracles, and pointing them out to you – especially when you were not aware of them before – helps to expand your knowledge and appreciation of the world around you. Just knowing makes you better. Enjoy!

Have You Ever Seen a Nuclear Explosion?

We are not asking whether you have seen one in the movies or on television. Have your eyes, even once, been

Bombing of Nagasaki

blinded by a light too bright to look at, with the shadow behind you cast by a ball of almost unimaginably titanic energies whose internal temperature is measured in the millions of degrees? Have you felt the explosion's heat on your exposed skin, knowing that if you were to stay exposed for too long you would blister and burn?

But wait, before you answer that question, understand that you *have* personally seen a nuclear explosion! Its rays have darkened your skin. Indeed, you have seen thousands, if not millions of them. You've watched them with others, including family and friends.

These explosions vary in size from really, really large, to relatively small, with the closest one just that.

If you have not yet figured out the riddle, here are a few hints: the explosions can be seen in the daytime and at night; in the morning and evening; when growing up, and during the last days of life. They cannot be seen when it rains or snows, however.

These very many nuclear explosions power the stars in the sky, with the nearest one known as "Sol," or simply the Sun. Each star, including our Sun, is a huge ball – an ongoing nuclear explosion that will last billions of years. Living in the light of nuclear explosions – as life on Earth does – might be considered an everyday miracle.

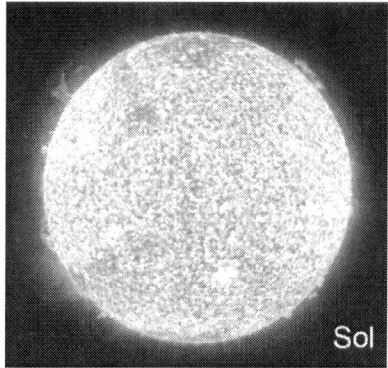

Sol

Sit Still

How many times have you heard your mother say "sit down and be still?" To do so is a miracle; though not because you might always fidget.

Our planet is sometimes called the third rock from the Sun. From that perspective, it is easy to understand that, while you may think you always can move forward, fall back, or stand in place – the last is impossible. You, of course, *know* that the Earth is spinning on its axis, so even sitting asleep in your favorite lounge chair, you are moving at almost 1,000 miles per hour around the Earth's circumference. Quick question here, which way are you moving??? Come on, no cheating. One would think that

it is easy to know which way you are moving –
particularly at that speed!

Of course, you might argue that what is making you
hesitate before giving your answer is the fact that we are
all simultaneously moving in other directions, too. Our
planet is not just spinning on its axis; it also orbits the
Sun. The Earth moves around the Sun at about 67,000
miles per hour. What's more, our entire solar system is
orbiting our Milky Way Galaxy's center at about 500,000
miles per hour, and our entire Galaxy is racing through
the expanding Universe. Despite all of this high-speed
motion, we here on Earth feel none of it. Are you getting
dizzy yet?

Your mother might very well consider your sitting still
to be a miracle. But the everyday reality of how you
cannot sit still may be even more so.

Reach Out and Touch

Put your hand on your kitchen table. You can feel its
smooth surface, the grain of the wood, perhaps even the
crumbs left behind. As you press down, you feel its solid
structure. What is unusual about touching a table?

Your hand, the table, indeed all the things around you
– even the air you breathe – are mostly not there. Their
solidity is an illusion; their substance, specious. From
that perspective, touching something is impossible, as
you should expect your hand to simply pass through the
table.

What the...?

In answer, you know that everything is made up of
stuff. For your hand, this includes skin, muscles, bones,
blood, and nerve tissues. Each of these substances can
be broken down into their molecules, and these to their

elemental parts, down to individual atoms. Let's look at the simplest of these atoms, Hydrogen. Each of its atoms is made of two parts, a nucleus circled by an electron. In Hydrogen's case, the nucleus consists of a single proton. The atom is very, very small, and yet it is still made up of mostly empty space.

Here's a *picture*. If a Hydrogen nucleus was the size of a cherry, and was floating at the 50th floor of the Empire State Building, then its single electron would be tracing out an orbit touching the ground floor and the building's peak some 50 stories away. There would be nothing else in that entire space, but space. This is true of any atom, so the image of two virtually empty spaces passing through each other conveys a sense of the mystery of why a hand *touching* a table seems impossible.

The intent here is not to give you a complete education on physics or any of the sciences, but to leave crumbs leading to the wonder of the world around us. To amplify this particular one, here are two other images at the far opposite of the *size* scale. The Hubble Space Telescope orbiting above has taken many pictures showing entire galaxies colliding. These galaxies consist of literally billions of stars and planets. Amazingly, despite the collision, the individual stars rarely actually

Two Galaxies Colliding

collide.   Instead, the galaxies simply pass through and around one another. Again, the reason is that despite the massive size of stars and planets, galaxies are mostly empty space.

This is our family portrait. It is the only real picture (actually a collection of pictures) taken of our entire Solar System.   The collage was snapped by the Voyager I

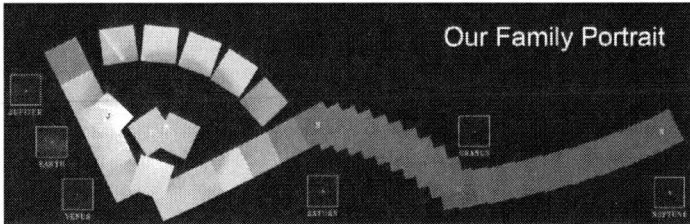
Our Family Portrait

spacecraft on its incredible trek beyond our Sun's domain. It proportionally depicts the planets and the Sun as they actually look from afar. The Sun is the bright spot near the letters "EV" which themselves indicate the location of Earth and Venus. As you can see, despite the enormous size of the Sun and of the larger planets like Jupiter (J) and Saturn (S), our Solar System is mostly empty space.

Clap On…

…goes the words of an advertisement for a remote-controlled light switch.   But sometimes clapping can trigger something interesting enough that it, upon examination, merits inclusion here.

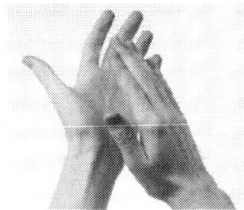

This chapter began asking about your personal experience with nuclear explosions – something all sane people fear. The huge outpouring of energies from such blasts can be measured in the tens, if not hundreds of millions of tons of TNT. Yet, the first demonstration of scientists' ability to control atomic reactions took place in an old squash court under a university stadium – almost in defiance of the genie-in-the-bottle about to be uncorked. That this initial experiment by Enrico Fermi in 1942 took place in Chicago illustrates the innocence then prevailing. The U.S. Department of Energy history captures this:

"Unlike most reactors that have been built since, this first one had no radiation shielding and no cooling system of any kind. Fermi had

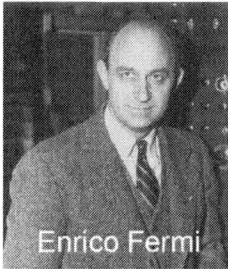
Enrico Fermi

convinced Arthur Compton that his calculations were reliable enough to rule out a runaway chain reaction or an explosion, but, as the official historians of the Atomic Energy Commission later noted, the "gamble" remained in conducting a possibly catastrophic experiment in one of the most densely populated areas of the nation!"

Lessons were learned from seeing theory become reality while others were learned from accidents that happened. The costs and risks, uses and benefits of reactors have become better known. Reactors have been built to drive aircraft carriers and submarines; to create isotopes for use in medicine and weapons; and most visibly, as commercial power plants to provide electricity.

What most reactors have in common is that their energies are used, well, basically, to boil water. To put this in perspective consider what is happening within the reactor. Atoms are splitting, and as they do so their particles strike other atoms and cause them to split. This splitting generates heat. Reactors are designed to transfer this heat to their cooling systems, much as an automobile engine's heat is transferred to be cooled in its radiator. A Nuclear Reactor's heat is used to heat water which is allowed to become steam and is then directed against *fan blades* making them turn. These turbine blades are connected to a shaft which rotates. The shaft can have a propeller at its distant end – as in a ship – or it can turn the massive coils of wire in a generator which creates electricity.

Whether electricity is created by a nuclear reactor's heat or from a coal or gas fire's heat, the electricity is the same. This is also true when the generator is turned by water stored behind a dam or by wind – as well as when the sun shines on a solar panel, though the process of generation is different. The electricity is sent from these generators, through a wire, to those who need it. It is typically sent at very high voltages (think water-pressure) and those voltages will be reduced by devices called transformers before the electricity reaches its final destination – whether to turn a motor or light a bulb.

The technology needed to store commercial electricity does not yet exist. Electricity flows at the speed of light from the generator to the user where, after use, it flows back into the Earth beneath our feet – *ground*. Yes, there are batteries, but these play such a minor role in the provision of commercial electricity as to be invisible. When your light switch is turned on, the power that is flowing in the grid has a new place to go. That means that the voltage in the grid drops just a little.

Voltage drops can be measured, and when they become significant they trigger a response. You can think of it as a voltage meter determining that more power is needed. It then tells a power source to go to work; perhaps it is a gas turbine. There a valve opens, and gas is injected into a boiler, where it flares and heats water to steam...until more electricity is created. The process can also work in reverse, reducing the flow of electricity into the system.

You might consider this when you next enter a dark room and clap your hands to turn on the lights. You may be signaling to a nuclear reactor that its control rods need to raise or lower. Clapping your hands may be how you are triggering one of the most fundamental reactions in nature – the power that creates atom bombs.

En-LIGHT-enment

Albert Einstein determined that: $E = mc^2$, which is mathematical shorthand for: *Energy equals Mass times the Speed of Light squared.* In simple terms, he realized that every bit of matter in the universe (e.g. atoms, rocks, you) can be converted into energy (e.g. heat, radiation, light) and vice-versa.

Since Einstein's famous equation includes the *speed of light squared*, which is a very, very big number, it shows how a very small amount of matter, say one ounce of Uranium, can be converted into an enormous amount of energy. In fact, only $1/40^{th}$ of an ounce of Uranium was converted into energy over Hiroshima, Japan in 1945 to create the explosion obliterating that city and killing nearly 100,000 people.

Scientists came up with a way to count very small things. Avogadro's number is the number of molecules in a *mole* of a substance. That is approximately 6.022×10^{23} molecules. What this really means is that there are 602,200,000,000,000,000,000,000 pieces of a thing in just one of the fundamental measures of stuff – one mole.

That huge number of molecules that makes up a mole is only about as big as a pea. Molecules are themselves made up of atoms, which are themselves made up of other, small sub-atomic particles, and then smaller ones yet.

When one of these particles is converted into energy as described by Einstein's equation, it produces a very small amount of energy. But since there are so many particles in something the size of a pea, the total amount of energy released by converting something that size is enormous.

Einstein has thus given us a miracle here by showing how a dizzyingly large number of particles so impossibly small in size can generate an incredible amount of energy.

Something from Nothing

NASA placed the Hubble Space Telescope in orbit above the Earth in 1990. Since then, it has peered into the depths of the universe giving us a glimpse of distant sights as they were billions of years ago – the time it took for their light to reach the telescope. We have seen galaxies whose shapes wonder the imagination; stars being born and dying; and have discovered new planets. Black holes, the stuff of science fiction, have been confirmed. The Hubble has even been focused on areas of the sky where there was *nothing*.

Using the Hubble is expensive; there are many demands for its resources. So taking pictures of *nothing* was a risk. But astronomers were determined to see what, if anything, they could find in what was thought to be an empty piece of sky. The area that the telescope examined was tiny: if you hold a grain of sand at arm's length above you, the area of the sky photographed is roughly the size covered by that one grain. But, when the astronomers reviewed the pictures, there was more than a bit of astonishment. Some 3,000 galaxies were found! Even strained to its maximum magnification covering only a miniscule portion of the sky, the telescope still found its aperture filled with galaxies – with each containing countless billions of stars.

These are the actual Hubble images from what is called its *Ultra-Deep Field Survey*. The image on the left indicates the area of interest (that small box) where there was *nothing*. The image on the right is what Hubble found in that small space!

Icebergs Do Float

Our physical world, Mother Earth, is also replete with miraculous and seemingly fortuitous mechanisms. As you know, water is a key feature of our world. It nurtures life, controls the weather, and moderates the environment – it is, quite literally, the lubrication that makes the engine of our planet work. It also has some very unusual properties which allow it to do these things.

After a hard day's work, you might crave a cold drink: a tall glass of ice water, or perhaps iced tea. You can almost feel how the floating cubes will chill the liquid and make drinking it so wonderful. But why does the ice

float? It is, after all, simply solid water. Most elements and chemicals in the Universe become more dense as they get colder. Water does that too. But, as the temperature is further reduced, water freezes and becomes ice. Solids are usually more dense than when in liquid form: iron is denser as a solid, so is rock denser than lava. But ice is not denser than water. That's why it floats. If it was denser, it would sink and your ice cubes would be sitting at the bottom of your glass. This does not seem to be a problem until you consider the bigger picture.

Ice can be found on the ocean, great sheets of it covering thousands of square miles of the Arctic Oceans, atop lakes, and as huge icebergs. If this were not the case – if ice sank, it would fall to the bottom of the body of water. There the sun would never have a chance to melt it. Each year, more ice would form. Eventually, and perpetually, every body of water would fill with ice and our planet would become a frozen waste.

Isn't it lucky that your ice cubes float – or just amazingly wonderful?

It's Full of Stars

We owe the telescope's namesake, Edwin Hubble, another debt. It was he who first discovered a galaxy outside our own. It was he who first realized the true scope of our Universe in which our Milky Way Galaxy is just one of some hundred billion galaxies each with hundreds of billions of stars.

Edwin Hubble

In his later work, he discovered that the farther away these galaxies were, the faster they were moving away from us through space – which has since become *Hubble's law*. He did this by employing something with which we are all familiar: how the pitch of a car horn approaching, changes as it passes. This is called the Doppler Effect. However, in his case, he used changes in the color of light instead of changes in the pitch of sound. His law then provided, at last, the proof of the idea that, at one time in the past, the entire Universe was created in a giant explosion, the *Big Bang*. Some 14 billion years later, the observable Universe is about 94 billion light years across and continues to expand. Current thinking is that the Universe will continue to expand forever.

Conclusion

Did the Big Bang happen? What caused it? What existed before it? Asked another way, what happened in the time before time began? And, as intriguingly, what lies beyond those farthest galaxies? There are many other such questions, but no factual answers. Believers in a Deity may point to the Bible's opening chapter, "Let there be light," but no matter whether you are a believer or not, these are more of our everyday miracles.

The list of everyday miracles is long and will surely contain that the New York Giants defeated the New England Patriots in two Super Bowls. More seriously, it would certainly include conception and growth; the workings of the body; and of any of the world's systems: water, weather, or whatever. Forests and oceans would be included. It might also include those things which are not as tangible such as: an idea, friendship, art or music.

Curiosity is a hallmark of human intelligence. It is our birthright to explore that which is beyond the horizon.

Some conjecture that, since we are part of the Universe, our thirst for knowledge and drive for understanding is actually the Universe trying to understand itself. For millennia, the human condition has been enhanced and enriched through the results of our explorations. And as the playwright and poet, T. S. Elliot once ventured:

> *"We shall not cease from exploration*
> *And the end of all our exploring*
> *Will be to arrive where we started*
> *And know the place for the first time."*

These few miracles may have amused you. Hopefully, they made the point that a close examination of virtually anything will amaze. Perhaps they stimulated your imagination. Most importantly, it is hoped that you will be motivated to look about you and discover the miracle of many other seemingly mundane things around you. It will only make you better.

It is fitting to end this chapter with the words of the astrophysicist, Sir Arthur Eddington:

"The Universe is not just stranger than we imagine, it is stranger than we can imagine."

Chapter 13 – AGE OF THE COMPUTER

You may consider yourself a computer-phobe, believing that you are not capable of learning anything about them. Nonsense! Getting an understanding of computers is not a big deal. There are a couple of things that you need to know. This chapter and the next give them to you, and do not demand a huge amount of memorization from you. A first read of the chapters will do much for you, and if you choose to re-read them, do so to get more. Suddenly you will find yourself with abilities you never had before because you will have a starting place from which to understand technical problems that seem to come at you constantly.

The reality of today, not just of tomorrow, is that the world is now *digital*. If you don't understand that, it is explained later. Digital Computers are at the center of the technical foundation of the modern world. Other elements include information (whose explosion is accelerating) and communications (which have become inescapable). The ever-more-powerful computers, limitless information, and ubiquitous communications surround, if not overwhelm all of us. They have affected every facet of modern life and their effect will only grow. Woe unto the person who ignores the influence of these three superpowers of the age.

This chapter and the next provide some, but not too much, information about computers. Knowing about them will strengthen your personal foundation so that you are able to better deal with many other things you will encounter in life.

These chapters also provide perspective so that you can arrange the seemingly random pieces into a complete mosaic and be able to see it and understand it for what it is. Here you will get a sense of what the critical computer technologies are; how far they have come; and about their near-distant future. Some of these forecasts are almost beyond belief, but that does not make them less true – you will see some surprising future ballparks. Being aware of them will put you a step ahead and makes you prepared to benefit from them.

Some who use computers argue that people do not need to understand how they work. They cite cars and TVs as examples of technology that we simply expect to work, without knowing or caring how. A common joke is that when an automobile engine stalls we do not need to close all the windows, get out and lock the doors before re-starting. While humorous, this analogy is false. A Ford Model T from almost one hundred years ago had four wheels, seated 4-6 adults, and used a gasoline-powered internal combustion engine. People used their cars to go on trips at the wondrous speed of about 45 mph.

1912 Ford Model T Roadster

Compare that to your last automobile trip. Passenger cars have progressed far less than you might imagine.

Electronic computers' progress has been different. Though invented only a few decades after the auto, their progress has been meteoric. Seventy years ago, the first general purpose computer weighed 60,000 pounds. It had 18,000 vacuum tubes installed in a metal housing eight feet tall and eighty feet long. Today, your watch has a hundred times the power of this massive device.

ENIAC, c1950

Wait. You just read a lie. Do you even wear a watch anymore – other than because you once did and don't want to throw it out? Wristwatches have been replaced several times now, with each generation of technology a hundred times more powerful than the last. From their beginning, computers have grown in power by more than a factor of a *Million!*

Required Technologies

Computers weren't created in a vacuum. There are many sciences and technologies that had to be developed before electronic digital computers would see the light of day. These technologies are not just important factors in the development of computers, but are the basis for much in our modern society. Read now about some technologies that were developed around a fundamental force of nature: Electricity.

Electricity can be thought of as a form of energy resulting from the instantaneous movement of electrons

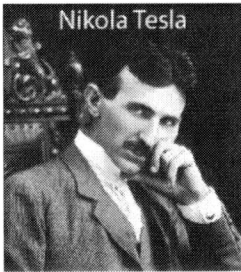
Nikola Tesla

through a wire. The first electric distribution *system* was built by Thomas Edison in downtown Manhattan, New York. Its electricity flowed in only one direction. It went from Edison's generators, through the lights it was powering (making the filament glow) and then into the ground. This type of system is called **Direct Current** (DC). Later, Nikola Tesla and George Westinghouse found that it was much more efficient to move electricity across large distances using **Alternating Current.** AC (as the name implies) alternates the current, sending it out, then reversing the direction and bringing it back. This reversal typically

George Westinghouse

repeats 60 times per second in today's systems.

All electricity today moves from the generating station to your house via AC. Most of the appliances, tools, lights, etc. in your house use it. However, electronic products – televisions, telephones, stereos, and, most especially, computers do not. They use DC, converting the power coming into your house by using those little black cubes that you plug in the wall. Inside those cubes are devices called **rectifiers** that do the actual conversion. In the case of personal computers, their built-in **power supply** does this, and also carefully regulates the voltage so that all the components inside the box get exactly what they need (computer components are very sensitive to fluctuations in voltage).

Little more than 100 years ago, electricity was only to be found in the laboratory. There, Thomas Edison would imprison a filament's glow in glass. He would later release it to the world – the incandescent light-bulb – for mankind to use to banish the night. Then, at the dawn of the electric age, scientists throughout the world experimented on and learned of electricity's properties. Engineers followed using this knowledge to build. Their first devices only did simple things: **diodes** allow current only to flow in one direction; **capacitors** (originally called condensers) store current; and **resistors** restrict the flow of current. An interesting one is called an **oscillator**, vibrating crystals which precisely regulate frequency and so are often found in electric clocks. Many of these devices were originally built as **vacuum tubes**.

The engineers then took the next step, soldering individual parts onto what came to be called **circuit-boards**. Each used electricity to create what would not-too-far-before be considered magic: seeing objects from a great distance (radar) and transmitting sound and pictures across even greater distances (telephones, radios and televisions). The first half of the twentieth century was marked by an explosion of such inventions. This creative output accelerated in the second half – an era which came to be defined by the development of just one type of specialized circuit. This circuit was one that effectively executed an instruction by itself – a computer circuit, of which you will learn more.

Transistors

The early computing machines were enormous – weighing 20 to 30 tons. They consumed huge amounts of power, were noisy, and were so hot that each required a massive cooling system. Hugely expensive – some cost millions of dollars – they were attended by a small army of maintenance technicians. Their tens of thousands of

vacuum   tubes   were   prone   to   failure;
typically one to two thousand tubes were replaced each
month.

All this was about to change with the invention of the
transistor. Its impact is so fundamental that it can be
compared to the invention of banking, or of the printing
press, or even of fire!
Transistors are made of
tiny pieces of semi-
conductor materials like
Silicon and Germanium.
Normally, these materials
are neither Insulators nor conductors of electricity. They
only allow electricity to pass under certain conditions.
When assembled in very specific ways, these materials
create the miracle that is our modern age.

Typical Vacuum Tubes

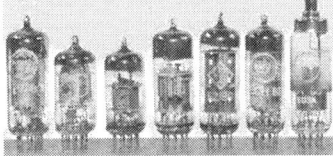

Transistors are hardier, easier to manufacture,
require much less electricity to operate, and can operate
at speeds much faster than vacuum tubes. But it is the
combination of their small size and low cost that truly
distinguishes them. Initially, ten transistors could be built
on a chip for the cost of one vacuum tube – 35¢. This
figure soon became one
hundred, then a thousand.
Today the number of
transistors on a chip can be
in the range of a Billion
(1,000 x 1,000 x 1,000) – for
the same 35¢ (of course,
the complexity of the
largest chips makes its actual cost higher). Each chip is
far smaller than your fingernail. Astonishingly, the limits
to transistor manufacturing have not been reached!

Typical Transistors

The ability to replace tubes with transistors was only one part of the incredible shrinkage of the physical size of computers. As the components became miniaturized, so did the wires themselves. These two factors mean that the physical limits to the increase in computing power – the number of tubes and the wires connecting them – were eliminated. The manufacturing process that creates many joined transistors on a single chip of silicon delivers

Intel 8008 Microprocessor

an **integrated circuit** (IC). In 1971, Intel introduced the first **microprocessor IC** – a general-purpose, *computer-on-a-chip* with an initial cost in dollars. This marked an important milestone in the proliferation of computers by allowing for the production of affordable and relatively compact *personal computers* (PCs).

We now have all of the key technologies needed to construct a computer. The next step will occur in our next chapter.

Laws

Technology continues to advance dramatically. One way to become familiar with these changes is to learn some of the *laws* that have been formulated to describe those changes. Of course, those offered here capture only a sense, but they do encapsulate a degree of truth – and that in itself, if understood, gives you a leg up on those for whom our technological world is only a mystery.

The first deals with computers; the next two are about communications. Then comes economics as it applies to technology and finally there are some warnings which might be of interest.

Moore's Law: Chips are shrinking and have always done so. Gordon Moore, the co-founder of Intel, noted that the number of transistors that can be placed on a chip would double every two years. This forecast has held steady for 40 years. The increase in density over that time can be expressed mathematically as 2^{20}! Stated another way, where there were only about 2,000 transistors on a chip in 1971, today there are about 10,000,000,000 which makes the cost of each one less than the cost of a single character printed in the Sunday *NY Times*!

Gilder's Law: George Gilder, a prolific author, wrote that the bandwidth of communication systems triples every 12 months. On a practical level, where a communications link into your home could once transmit only 120 characters per second, today, the number is measured in the millions. This example does not, however, address the major communications pathways that have been built, or that are being planned – whose capacity is far greater. This law explains why it is possible to relocate call centers across the Earth – that's a joke – albeit a sad one to those who have lost their jobs as they have been shipped far overseas.

Metcalfe's Law: The inventor of *Ethernet* (which is in the next chapter), Robert Metcalf stated that the value of being connected to a network grows exponentially with the number of connections available to you, i.e. as the square of the number. He continued his observation noting that the cost per user will remain the same or shrink. In practical terms, two connections deliver a benefit of four; four connections deliver a benefit of sixteen; ten…, a hundred. The Internet now has millions of connections, all available to you – do the math.

Wriston's Law: A giant of banking and finance, Walter Wriston predicted the rise of electronic financial networks. He said that both money and ideas, when freed to travel at the speed of light will go where wanted and stay where well-treated. His prediction described how the world's technology centers change so quickly.

Murphy's Law: There are so many technical versions of the adage: "anything that can go wrong, will." Here are a few, without commentary: "A computer makes as many mistakes in two seconds as 20 men working 20 years." "The attention span of a computer is only as long as it electrical cord." "The only perfect science is hindsight." "There is never time to do it right, but always time to do it over." ...and perhaps the favorite: "Multi-million dollar technology is worthless in the hands of morons."

Thank You

To stand on the shoulders of giants is to benefit from those who pass before; they who did not have the advantage of 20/20 hindsight. That is true of you in your life. You do not know what you may be thanked for, but know that continuing forward is the direction you must continue to forge. The following list has just a few of the many giants whose hard work is today benefiting the world:

Charles Babbage: An English inventor, mechanical engineer, and philosopher. He is considered the father of the computer. He is credited with inventing the first mechanical computer – but this was a hundred years before electricity, so his machines were designed to be powered by steam.

Herman Hollerith: An American statistician, he is considered by many to be the father of automatic computation. He chose the punched card as the medium to store information. While working for the U.S. Census Bureau, he developed a mechanical tabulator to process the millions of pieces of information generated by the 1890 census. Years later, the firm he founded merged with three others to become IBM.

Alan Turing: An English mathematician, cryptanalyst, and computer scientist, he formalized the concept of the *algorithm* (a step-by-step procedure for calculations) and of computing using his *Turing Machine*. He created one of the first designs for a stored program computer and is considered to be the father of computer science.

George Stibitz: invented the first modern digital computer while working at Bell Labs. He built it from old electromechanical relays normally used for switching telephone calls, flashlight bulbs, batteries, tin strips, and wires. He sat down at his kitchen table to fiddle, and later, named his machine the Model K in honor of that table.

John von Neumann: An astoundingly versatile Hungarian-American mathematician who was an early computer scientist. His contributions to the nascent field will be long remembered, including the very architecture still used.

Betty Snyder Holberton, Jean Jennings Bartik, Kathleen McNulty Mauchly Antonelli, Marlyn Wescoff Meltzer, Ruth Lichterman Teitelbaum and Frances Bilas Spence: These six ladies were the original programming team of the ENIAC computer.

Gene Amdahl: A Norwegian-American computer architect and inventor of the IBM 360 computer, the most successful machine of its era. He later founded his own company to build even-more advanced machines. His is Amdahl's law, still used to forecast the benefits of parallel computing.

John Bardeen, William Shockley, and Walter Brattain: were three American physicists at Bell Laboratories in 1947 who were the co-inventors of the *transistor* and were jointly awarded the Nobel Prize in Physics for their accomplishment.

Rear Admiral Grace Hopper: Needed an underweight exemption to enlist in the U.S. Military, but her true heft was her mind. She was called Amazing Grace for her breadth of accomplishments, including creating the COBOL language and more prosaically, calling computer program errors *bugs*.

Steven Jobs: An American businessman, inventor, and visionary, he co-founded the Apple Computer Company. His innovative designs and

use of a *graphical user interface* on his Macintosh PCs —
which uses a mouse instead of a line of typed commands
— drove much of future PC designs. His vision and drive
shaped the consumer electronics industry and has
resulted in morphing the concept of a personal computer
to include such things as iPads and iPhones.

Men and women from around the world, these and
so many others are the shoulders upon which we stand.
You have so far seen the technologies used as the basis
for computer design, learned some of the laws that shape
the industry, and met a few of the giants who've set the
pace. More critically, you've been given an appreciation
of the significant importance of computers to modernity
in general and, more pointedly, to your life. The next
chapter will show that the computer's secrets need not
be so mysterious after all.

Chapter 14 – COMPUTERS EXPOSED

Computers are not magic machines, yet many people fear these amazingly powerful, increasingly necessary, yet surprisingly brainless boxes. Computers are truly astounding, but they need not be full of mystery. Their depths are fathomable, and their secrets are not so dark. You have already seen what goes into one: electricity, electronic components, circuit boards, transistors, and ICs. Now take the next step and put it all together. Build a computer!

Executing Instructions

The idea of a machine for doing math is not new. One type of calculator is over 5,000 years old – the abacus. Others were built which use changing physical quantities (the length of a stick in a slide rule, or the position of a gear in a mechanical adding machine). These are called **analog** devices. But today's electronic circuits are a world away from those. They use only one of two possible conditions – one or zero, on or off. They are **digital**.

Engineers took their early, simple circuits, modified them, and built something called a **gate.** This special circuit allows electrical current to pass through only under certain conditions. One type allows electricity to flow only if it come from this wire AND that one, too. Similar **logic** is used for the other types of gates like OR and NOR. This allows the computer to *make decisions*.

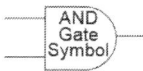

Many unique electronic parts have been invented. You can think about these as if they were different types of Lego toys in a box. Engineers choose from them to build new circuits. Some of these are intended to be in a computer to perform an **instruction**.   Each of these circuits does only one simple thing.   It may move some data from here to there, or add two numbers.   All together, these circuits are the **instruction set** of the computer. They do practical work – they are the brains of a computer.

Their early uses were military such as artillery ballistics calculations. These would otherwise have taken several rooms-full of mathematicians years to complete. The work of these early machines began in the 1930s and continued through the 1940s.   Their work was so important that it was kept secret during the Second World War.

Once the circuits for individual instructions existed, something was needed to tie them all together to perform complex jobs. A **program** is a list of instructions. It literally and simply is a collection of instructions needed to do some more complex job.   Since computers can perform individual instructions very, very quickly, even complex jobs can also be done much faster than by hand. But remember, computers do not think. The machines are rather, well, dumb.   They do exactly what the program tells them to do – no more – no less. And if you tell them to delete all of your data, or to drive off a cliff, they will. If the programmer lists the steps incorrectly, the program might not run at all, or if it does, you have what has become known as a **bug**.

The CPU

The first programs consisted of the multiple circuits wired one to the next. Changing the program required physically rewiring the machine so that instruction circuits would run in a different order. Effectively, they programmed with soldering irons. This is called being **hard-wired**.

In **Programmable computers,** the program is written as a series of codes; each instruction has a unique name or number. Instead of wiring circuits together, the coded program is put into memory, and brought to the **processor** one instruction at a time. Each instruction circuit is in the processor, along with other specialized ones that ensure the correct instruction circuit will get run. The **processor** also keeps track of what is next so programs do not need to be strictly sequential. They can repeat instructions in loops until certain conditions are met.

There are special places in the processor called **registers**. They hold the information to be worked upon by any instruction circuit. These are the places where the data gets moved to and from memory when needed. There are very few of them. Early computers had four; the most advanced computers now have 128. This may seem like a bottleneck, but data is continually moved into and out of these registers from other types of memory holding vastly more data.

The **clock**, regulates the speed of the individual pulses of electricity flowing through the instruction circuits. It forces everything in the computer to march in lock-step, one instruction at a time. One of the earliest computers, the Mark I, operated at 833 instructions per second. This is a little slower than the billions per second computers now typically do.

Together, the processor, the control unit, the clock, and the registers make up the **Central Processing Unit, or CPU**. It is the heart of any computer system.

Typical Computer CPU

All of the hardware which is part of the computer system is called, well, **hardware**. In contrast, programs exist only on paper or in the computer's memory, so they are called **software**.

Binary

Digital computers store and manipulate everything as **binary data**, a series of zeros or ones, each called a **bit**. Eight bits grouped together are called a **byte**. In turn, bytes are combined into **words** that have 16, 32, or 64 bits each. The larger the word size, the more data can be pumped through the computer for each clock cycle. A single byte (8-bits) can represent the integers 0 to 255 (2^8 unique numbers).

```
1 0 0 1 1
0 0 1 1 1
1 1 0 1 0
```

Different coding schemes are used for negative, floating point, etc. numbers, and for non-numeric characters. One popular one is the American Standard Code for Information Interchange, ASCII. This assigns the English alphabet (both upper and lower case), numerical digits, the special characters (like $, %, and *) and other symbols to a number between 0 and 255. The processor uses the code to determine what you are referring to and displays it accordingly.

Data Storage

Binary *words* are stored in a computer's *memory* and accessed when needed. Memory can take several forms. Some are volatile – they are emptied when power is removed. Others are called non-volatile – they keep the data no matter what (hard drives, CD's, DVD's, etc.). Typically, volatile memory is kept on special chips on the circuit board called *Random Access Memory, RAM*. Early computers had a capacity of only 96 words in RAM. At current writing, computers can have over sixteen gigabytes (16 followed by 9 zeroes!) of RAM. The data stored in memory must ultimately be brought into the heart of the processor, copied into volatile memory locations – the few *registers* described earlier.

Internals of a Hard Disk Drive

Other types of long-term storage were invented to keep data safe when power was off, and to hold more data – a lot more. Early machines used punched cards. These had 80 columns (later ones, 96). Cards were fed into the computer one at a time – millions of them were needed for some programs. These were slow and error-prone.

Alternatives were developed. These included magnetic tape and disks. The data stays on the magnetic medium until erased or written over. Disk drives were first developed in 1956 by IBM and were the size of refrigerators. Eventually, they were miniaturized. When the PC was first developed in the late 1970's, it employed an external disk drive. This feature was imbedded in the very structure of how those machines work. In fact, the original Operating System designed for these computers was called the **Disk Operating System** (DOS). **Floppy disks** were introduced as cheap, portable and easy-to-use long-term storage, but they were slow and limited in capacity. They are rarely seen today. **Hard disk drives** hold a lot more data and are much faster. They use solid platters which spin very fast.

Other types of data storage devices have become common. CD's and DVD's are optical media – they store data permanently as burned dots on a disk of metal covered in plastic. A laser is used to read and write these dots. They hold a lot of data, but not as much as a hard drive and they are not nearly as fast. Thumb drives (aka flash drives) and memory cards (like SD and Compact Flash) are not really drives at all. They have non-volatile chips inside. With no moving parts, they are reliable and easy to use but are somewhat expensive and limited in size.

Communications

There are many types of external devices that can be plugged into a computer. Usually, these devices are used to get data into or out of the computer. Printers are used to print text, graphics, and photos. They can include the ability to copy, scan, and even FAX.

Most computers today use a keyboard and mouse (or other pointing device like a trackball) to get the user's info and commands into the CPU. The **Universal Serial Bus** interface, or USB, connects all of these devices to the computer. The USB was designed to be user friendly and easy to use. Plug something in and the computer will automatically recognize it and set it up for immediate use. This is in contrast to the way it used to be in the 1980's when

USB Cable

serial and *parallel* busses made users go through complicated routines to get external devices to work.

Surprisingly, much of your computer's power is used to interface to the outside world. The Internet has made this connection critical. **Ethernet** is the interface of choice today when hard-wiring a computer to a network.

Ethernet Cable

It uses a simple cable to connect computers together through other devices called routers, modems, and hubs and can do so over long distances.

The latest way to connect computers to a network is wirelessly. There are no wires (except possibly to power the device). Everything is accomplished via radio signals. These types of connections are easy and common, but are slower than a wired connection and add security concerns.

Hardware Configurations

You now have an idea of how computers work. But there is another layer to understanding them. This is analogous to the Earth. It has its own systems (weather, water, etc.) but is also part of the Solar System which is itself, part of the Milky Way Galaxy, one among billions of galaxies. Earth is a participant in a larger system. Similar perspectives apply to computers. The following exposes you to a bit of the technical battles going on around you.

Single or multi-processor: Given that chips are cheap, should a computer use one CPU or many? Specialized processors can be used to handle specific tasks. In this approach, no single CPU does everything. An example of this is a computer with a Graphics Processing Unit (GPU). The GPU controls how images are displayed on your monitor. Now, take this idea and extend it. System designers choose between single or multi-processor approaches (dual, quad, etc.). Each increase their complexity and cost, but also increases functionality and speed.

Centralized or Distributed: There are many examples of structures that have evolved where more than a single level of control exists. This also applies to the data processing. Should there be a central computer system, widely distributed systems, or some combination? How should *mainframes*, *servers*, and *personal computers* interact? What should their roles and responsibilities be? This is becoming ever more complicated by new devices: the Personal Data Assistant (PDA), smart-phones, and someday, maybe even chips implanted in your head!

On a practical level, there are computers called ***servers*** (once called mini-computers) and those regarded as ***clients***. Servers give information and clients get it. When you go online to do a search on Google or Yahoo, your computer is contacting theirs to ask for something. Their *computer*, however, is actually a huge collection of large, very fast, server-machines. They store huge amounts of information and provide it to many clients at once. Your computer is the client. It collects and displays to you what is sent to it by the server. Much of the Internet is structured in this way.

Massively parallel: The millions of personal computers and their successors have burst upon the world. An innovative approach to solving problems that require enormous amounts of computing power is to use the unused computing power of lots and lots of machines. Problems are broken into component parts, each of which is given to a different computer. These kinds of systems have been built to include machines all around the world, and provide low-cost solutions to problems that have been thought impossible to solve.

The Cloud: Factories once each had their own huge electric generators. Now you get power from an outlet. No one knows, or cares, where electric power comes from. Similarly, for many years, companies built their own data centers with unique collections of computers and other equipment. That is now changing, as computer processing power is more and more from the ***cloud.*** This cloud is sometimes known as the ***Internet*** and also the ***Web*** (in the next chapter you will learn the difference). Those who draw on it rarely know or care where the physical computers are. The local computer on your desk is a client; it is acting as a *dumb* terminal. The application that you're using – say a word processor – runs on a remote computer while your data could be half the world away. This change may seem strange, particularly after just having purchased a new computer for the home, but it is one of the major trends we all face.

Software

Software are the programs that run on the hardware. It is roughly divided into two categories: Systems Software, the programs needed to manage the computer's internal resources; and Applications Software, intended to be used by users.

Operating Systems: The brain of the computer is a program. The **OS** contains all the ugly engineering that makes the system go. It lets you *talk* to the computer through a keyboard, mouse, etc. This is called the **User Interface**. Its **Input / Output (or I/O)** links to other components: disks, printers, routers, etc.). The OS also has an interesting little program called the **bootstrap**. Its sole function is to load the OS into memory when the computer first starts. There are many types of OS; they vary by manufacturer, type of computer, and capabilities needed. Today, they are best known as those supplied for personal computers. Microsoft is famous for its Windows brand of OS; Apple makes OS X for Macintosh and iOS for the iPad and iPhone. Others include Linux, BSD, and the granddaddy of them all, UNIX.

Utilities: There are many small functions that are used in the course of computer operations. These include: checking for viruses, sorting data or backing it up. These may be bundled with the OS or may be separate.

Applications: These are the programs that do what we want. The list is endless and includes many for all industries, professions, and activities. It is shocking to learn the very many uses computers have in: farming, manufacturing, law, medicine, science, research, sports, social interaction, entertainment, and government. More uses are being developed each day. Application software is what does the work, and often what provides the play: word processors, spreadsheets, Space Invaders, Mario, World of Warcraft, and all the rest.

There are also giant collections of applications – multiple programs designed to work together and deliver sophisticated functionality. They are known as **application suites**.

On the other end of the spectrum is the Mobile Application, or simply App.   Devices such as Smartphones, tablet computers (like the iPad), etc. use mini-applications to perform simple tasks.   This type of software is generally limited in scope and power when compared to classical computer software applications, but their purpose is the same.

Software as a Service (SaaS): A new way to use software is coming along with *cloud* computing. Programs that you want to use are run in the cloud. You do not have to buy them – you rent them, and the only charge is based upon usage.   This allows quick, inexpensive, and always up-to-date programs. These can deliver sophisticated functionality that would otherwise be prohibitively expensive.

Vaporware or Brochure-ware: Is a category of product, like the Brooklyn Bridge, that you never want to purchase.   When a supplier promises a new software application or capability but never seems to deliver it… that's vaporware.

There you have it. You now know, in some detail, all of the parts and pieces that make computers tick. There are many other facets and each contains tons of more detail than given here. If you are still curious about any of the above-mentioned topics … well, you know the answer.

Impact

You've seen the key technologies and components that go into making a computer work. You took a step back and looked at how these machines interact with each other and how software is used. Now let's take yet another step back and look at the *big picture*.

What impact has this amazing machine had on society? What might a future historian consider to be the most important and enduring effects on humanity as a result of this synthesis of silicon, electrons, and human ingenuity?

There is both bad and good for all things, and computers are no exception. But whatever your take is on their influence on society, you can't argue that computers have had a significant and very real impact. They are ubiquitous, they're everywhere, and there are a lot of them!

Entire generations have grown to adulthood only knowing a world of computers. Many of them are as comfortable with computers as their parents are with automobiles and their great-grandparents were with horses. They use technology seamlessly as if it was part of their existence – and it is. Children today are educated with computers in the classroom, often at each of their desks. Experiments have shown how toddlers can learn to use a mouse to play games on a PC before they can even speak.

The world has been transformed in many ways. Professionals often spend large parts of their day staring at a monitor. Tools like CAD (computer-aided design) have revolutionized the design of

CAD Drawing

complex engineered products. The retail world now must concern itself more with *bits* than with *bricks*. Distribution of products in the music, movie and book industries has been utterly transfigured. The consumer electronics industry bristles with new computer-controlled products with amazing functionality like HDTVs, smart-phones, digital cameras, GPS, etc. It seems like everything you buy has at least one computer chip in it.

Computer-controlled devices have enabled a more effective exploration of space and other hostile environments. Robotic drones do work that is too hazardous or distasteful for humans. Robots and other computer applications have greatly improved productivity in various industries – often at a cost of a laborer's job.

The forms of free expression that are available and in daily use by everyone, everywhere have never before been known. In writing this book, the word-processor brings amazing power and flexibility. Our thoughts flow (sometimes) unhindered by physical limitations like erasing ink, running out of paper or care for where in the chapter an individual thought would eventually go. With the advent of speech recognition, you will not even need to know how to type. Computers offer those with physical or mental challenges the ability to communicate and interact in ways never before possible.

Similarly, programs like Photoshop allow the creative among us to stretch their abilities in new directions – perhaps releasing a talent that would have otherwise never seen the light of day. Artists of various types are able to release their muses publically, untethered by the demands of business and finance. Web sites like *YouTube* and *Vimeo* act as outlets for these artists to contact their potential fan-bases worldwide thereby exposing humanity to the benefit of new and unheard of types of entertainment, thought, and experience.

Access to information is yet another empowering factor of computers via the Internet. We have a live tap into a huge collection of data. It isn't quite the sum of human knowledge yet, but this is coming. This information gives anyone the ability to do serious research, learn new things and, maybe most importantly, gain an appreciation of others around the world. Even those in far-off villages, isolated, disenfranchised or otherwise unconnected from civilization, can access this fount of human thought and creativity through satellites. Although censorship is always a concern, this free-flow of information has already had immense influence around the world.

Connectivity may turn out to be one of the most important, if maligned, impacts of computers. Texting, Tweeting, Emailing, and the like, have allowed us to communicate more effectively with those around us. But beyond that, Facebook, Twitter, and their ilk as well as various forums and blogs have given people around the world the gift of interconnection. They are able to freely trade ideas and news. This has already caused the fall of several dictatorial regimes witnessed in the so-called *Arab Spring*. This interconnectedness at once destroys walls constructed by power-hungry governments worldwide and bestows a new and welcome appreciation upon humanity: We are more alike than not. Despite the best efforts of those who would divide us, it may be the inhuman computer that brings us together and frees the individual to pursue his or her own happiness.

But there is a downside. All of this communicating and free-flow of information has made privacy a real concern. Identity theft is a very real problem. Viruses and other types of electronic crime destroy our data while causing lost productivity. The more dependence we have on computers the more we are at the mercy of those who would take them away.

There are those who have become addicted to computers through gaming, pornography, or social media.   Ironically,   there   are   growing   numbers   of youngsters who are bereft of normal social skills due to their obsession with online social media.

… And then the advantage of being always connected is sometimes a disadvantage.   Because we're always connected, there is no peace, no ability to get away from the constant stream of information, the never-ending interruptions, and the incessant demands for your attention. This is seen at home, on vacation, and even from restroom stalls, when calls and texts interrupt what should still be a very private time.

Conclusion

The computer's power comes from brute force. They are able to make billions of decisions per second and do so nearly flawlessly.   For activities that can be decomposed into procedural steps like playing Chess or performing repetitive tasks, computers are unbeatable. Humans have no hope in besting a well-designed computer in these kinds of jobs. To date, however, computers can't *think*. They cannot solve unexpected problems nor cope with unprogrammed events. They have a hard time with pattern recognition and have limited ability to intuit an answer. They can't *see* beyond their programming. And they are not sentient; they have no conscience. They have no moral or ethical compass.

The real question is, "Are these limitations a result of insufficiently sophisticated hardware and software, or is there an ineffable quality to the human mind that is forever beyond silicon-based intelligence?"   Many scientists are working on this question of *artificial intelligence*. They are making great strides in expanding the capabilities of computers to *mimic* human thought. IBM's *Watson* project's winning performance, famously seen on the TV game-show *Jeopardy*, is one example of these strides.

The far-future of the computer is anyone's guess. It is clear that they will continue to be a growing influence on our lives creating amazing new possibilities and troubling new concerns. Imagine the possibilities when computers will be able to communicate directly with our minds without the need for us to type, click or even speak – and they will. This could release even more fantastic avenues of expression. But will this eradicate the privacy of our own thoughts?

Perhaps the need for middle-men and corporate distribution networks for artists, composers, authors, performers, and moviemakers will be eliminated. Many types of retail establishments may disappear, replaced by websites. Commuting to work may become a thing of the past. We could simply stay at home and be just as *connected* to our employer, coworkers, customers, and suppliers as we would have been if co-located in one facility. We may have no reason to ever leave our homes!

Will computers eventually enhance and/or control every aspect of our lives? Will they replace our reality with one of their own generation (e.g. *The Matrix* or *Star Trek's* holodeck)? Will they ever be able to truly think, have a conscience, and be sentient (e.g. *I Robot*, *A.I.*, or Asimov's *Robot* series)? Are we clever enough to construct machines that will be more benefit than detriment? What happens when the machines are able to construct themselves?

You might want to think about the answers.

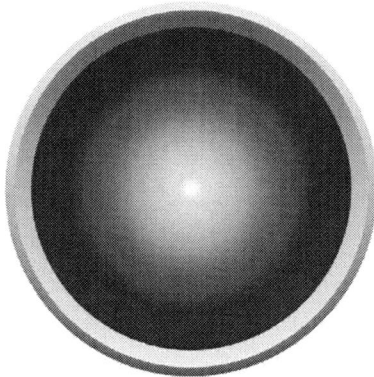

HAL 9000
From 2001: A Space Odyssey

Chapter 15 – THE INTERNET'S ORIGINS:

An Historical Perspective

In the last two chapters, you learned that computers are not quite as mysterious as you thought. You were shown some of their inner workings and technology. You saw how the information and communications revolutions changed the world upon the arrival of the Internet. But what is the Internet? How does it do the amazing things it does? Where did it come from?

The *Internet* aka, the *net*, the *World-Wide Web* or just the *Web* is changing everything. It brings the world into your office, home and even your vacation while flying, boating or back-packing. Many enjoy the benefits of electronic social contact through a virtual window which connects you with family, friends, and strangers. They can be in the next room, city, or across the globe.

But, its *dark-side* entices. It exposes our children to pornography, threatens privacy, and erases the distinction between work and family-time. Lives can be reduced to the single room they inhabit – a glowing computer screen used to interact with others who you never see. The crimes being committed are faceless and can assault without your even being aware that anything has happened.

What is this thing where surfers stay dry, browsers don't shop, and crawlers aren't used for fishing? Understanding the Web is important, useful, and not nearly as mysterious as it's sometimes thought to be. Grasping the fundamentals of the Web will help provide a foundation upon which to layer more and give you a basic understanding of what is to come.

In the twenty or so years since the term *Internet* first came to popular attention, millions of words have been written about it. But what is it? Can it be touched, smelled, or tasted? Must you read endlessly on the many complex technologies to understand it?

To describe the Internet technically, no matter how accurately, is to both take the easy path, and provide a poor answer. This approach is different: a journey through time where the ever-changing details matter less than the landscape. Before doing so, however, here is a short answer to the question of "What is the Web?" It is something easy to visualize and understand, if only by analogy.

The web can be thought of as being similar to the Earth's water system. The flow of information along the web's paths is like navigation along the world's waterways. Rain falls on the land. Tiny rivulets are formed and they grow: joining to form ever-larger streams until they emerge as rivers emptying into the oceans – all of which are joined. From any rivulet a continuous path can be traced to any other water. Even as water can be stored, transported, or transformed (into steam or ice), so can the information on the Web.

This simple image avoids both complexity and technology, is accurate, and is accessible. The veil of mystery surrounding the Internet is bypassed, not torn. The picture of information flowing along electronic rivers will be added to as we proceed to grow your footing in this essential thing. The stronger the foundation, the more impressive the structure it will support.

Accelerating Change

Each year, many who made our history are lost, so momentous events become ancient history to the newest generation. Even some of the best documented events, like the Holocaust, get questioned. A good way to begin learning about the World Wide Web is to look at the world as it was decades before the Web was even a dream. A reminder first: "History is an argument that never ends," so this review is given to provide insight – not to re-debate any detail about what influenced the creation of the Web.

At the dawn of the Twentieth Century, the world was almost unrecognizable from ours. It was agrarian; kings and queens ruled; the map of the world was replete with empires and colonies. Life was simpler – horsepower was fueled by oats, motivated by buggy whips, and needed shovels to clean up after.

Much of that is gone. Change reminds us that we are alive. But for every positive, there may be a negative; change can be benign or malignant – a stick can be a lever or a spear. We find, yet simultaneously lose. The telephone allows us to communicate with each other across vast distances, but interrupts at the most inopportune moments. Nuclear power promises pollution-free energy, but threatens radioactive contamination. Jet airplanes shrink the world, but remove the wonder of flight. Many of these changes can be heard with eyes shut: quiet waterwheels drowned by the sound of machinery; the scratching of quill feathers against paper by the keyboard's clatter; live music by amplified recordings; and the rhythms of horse and carriage by the automobile's roar.

A wide variety of technologies arrived to convulse and reshape everyone's lives, and the very fabric of society. The telephone, electric lights, movies, records, and the auto industry were all invented virtually at the same time! Ever-accelerating change obsolesced the new before the last could be bade fare-thee-well. Industrialization roared through the land powered by electricity, coal and oil, distributed by wire, conveyor, and pipeline – leaving their tailings, slicks, and clouds on the land, water, and air.

In the 20th century, men would wear pocket-watches on fobs; later, atomic clocks would broadcast time into bedrooms. Messengers would give way to video-conferencing across the world. Enjoying fireworks' rain of gun-powder-scented-debris would yield to fear of nuclear bursts delivered by Intercontinental Ballistic Missile. The Century would begin with great hopes for mankind only to have them repeatedly dashed.

Communism vs. Capitalism

The *hot* conflicts of the 20th century were world-wide, waged with weapons that could consume entire nations' populations. The cause of these conflicts was the fundamental difference between democracy and totalitarianism of one form or another. After millennia of dictatorial and often despotic rule, humanity began to embrace the democratic philosophies first developed by the ancient Greeks. The American and French revolutions led the way. They let the Genie out of the bottle, so to speak. Throughout the 20th century, populace government replaced monarchies, dictatorships, empires, and other centrally-run regimes. This shift was rarely done peaceably, as those in power often do not yield it without a fight.

The first half of the 20th century was marked by two devastating world wars. The one was a battle against many corrupt and morally bankrupt monarchies; the second against tyrannical and malevolent fascist regimes. The group of countries who defended democracy is still called the *Allies*. That term generally refers to the Western Democracies.

The defining struggle of the 20th century was between Communism and Capitalism. It lasted 84 years, but was only known as the *Cold War* for its latter half. This consumed most of the globe's attention as it threatened to utterly end civilization. The forces unleashed by this titanic struggle did have at least one positive outcome. They drove the creation of the Internet.

The struggle began with Karl Marx's words about the heartless side of industrialization. At the end of the 19th century, he wrote: "Capital is reckless of the health or length of life of the laborer, unless under compulsion from society." He advocated the creation of an entirely new system driven by principles that were almost religiously beautiful, his famous:

"From each according to his abilities, to each according to his needs."

Marx's Communist philosophy is naively flawed, however, and eventually grew to darken half the world before being discarded as a vast failure which withered the lives of millions.

Karl Marx

During the First World War, the power of the Communist Manifesto was recognized by the German Military. They literally used it as a weapon. Their High Command treated Marx's pupil, Vladimir Lenin, as if he were an infectious virus; they transported him in a sealed railroad car to be released into Russia. The operation caused a Revolution; it replaced the Czar with a Soviet regime who then removed themselves from the "War to end all Wars."

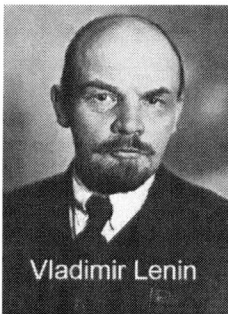
Vladimir Lenin

At War's end, America's President, Woodrow Wilson, was physically ill and unable to win support in his own country for a new international peacekeeping organization he championed, the League of Nations. Instead, the U.S. became isolationist, as it turned its back on Europe.

During America's *Roaring Twenties,* the Reds (as the Communists became known) consolidated their hold over what had been Russia. Europe's devastation gave U.S. industry a boost and its wealth exploded. Huge social movements followed, including prohibition on the

Woodrow Wilson

consumption of alcohol. This was openly defied. Crime flourished and took over Chicago and other cities.

The Stock Market Crash ended the era of rampant exuberance, replacing it with a dark pall. It is remembered by the *Black days* that entered Wall Street legend, especially Tuesday, October 29, 1929. The Dow Jones Industrial Index dropped 25% in just two days. A measure of the pain endured can be intimated by the fact that at its nadir, in 1932, the index was down by 89% – to 41 – from the peak reached just before the crash.

Time's passing teaches that the Great Depression was caused by badly misplaced policy. This is little consolation to those who were devastated then. A quarter of the workforce was thrown out of work. These numbered almost thirteen million people. Many had borrowed money to bet on a rising stock-market, assuming it would always rise. This *buying on margin*, as it was then known, is little different from the *leveraging* that would fuel the Real Estate Bubble of 2008. Those who forget history are condemned to repeat it!

The misery of the Depression Years was compounded by a severe drought. It was witnessed most vividly on *Black Sunday*, April 14, 1935, when bone-dry Great Plains soil was lifted into the air by a severe windstorm. The dust cloud was two miles high, and moved across the land at a mile a minute. The storm even darkened the sky over the Nation's Capital – arriving, as if on call, just as a soil conservation bill was being debated.

The Great Depression persisted despite President Roosevelt's many efforts. His unbridled optimism comes across in his first inaugural speech "We have nothing to fear, but fear itself" – unexpected from a man condemned to a wheelchair by polio. But the Great

Depression was not limited to America. It was felt worldwide and provided fertile fodder for ideologues and extremists to capture the hearts and minds of a desperate and hungry public.

World War II

The end of the Depression was marked by his most famous speech, beginning: "December 7, 1941, a date which will live in infamy..." These words unleashed United States' might in response to the sneak attack on our naval base at Pearl Harbor. Following the attack, the Japanese Admiral who commanded the mission, Admiral Isoroku Yamamoto, is purported to have said: "I fear all we have done is to awaken a sleeping giant and fill him with a terrible resolve." The United States ultimately took the lead in the fight against Japan's Prime

USS Arizona after Pearl Harbor Attack

Minister, Hideki Tojo and Germany's Fuhrer, Adolf Hitler.

The Second World War had been long anticipated. During the conference which drew up the peace treaty to formally end the First, or "War to end all Wars," the great Economist, John Maynard Keynes, publicly resigned from the British delegation. His protest over the terms of the proposed Peace Treaty was later put into an important book, *The Economic Consequences of the Peace*. While he and many others foresaw the coming war for which Germany and Japan prepared, the Allies hid behind their fortifications: the Americans their oceans; the British their Channel; and the French their Maginot Line.

The Soviet Union began the war allied with Germany, but switched sides after Hitler double-crossed them. The Allies' victory might have seemed preordained, given the might of the U.S. industrial base, but to all those thrown into the crucible of battle in 1940, the end was uncertain, if not dire. The war saw campaigns that spanned the globe: on the steppes and in the cities; in the air, and both on and beneath the oceans; across the desert, the mountains, and the jungle.

The Second World War spared none its horror. The atrocities perpetrated by Germany and Japan during the course of the war included *concentration* or death-camps, and the almost-as-bad slave camps. Almost two hundred thousand prisoners of war and impressed civilians died on just one forced-labor project. This project was the Japanese effort to build a railroad through the Thailand-Burma peninsula. It was to go through some of the most difficult terrain on Earth. The men died from disease, malnutrition, overwork – and deliberate torture. This tragedy was memorialized by the book, and later movie, *The Bridge over the River Kwai.*

As the war approached its end, the shelling and bombing of cities evolved. Their destruction was systematically scheduled. Roosevelt, Stalin, and Churchill met in the Ukraine to divide the post-war world into *spheres of influence.* But fundamental differences between the Capitalist and the Communist systems doomed their reconciliation to failure. Stalin saw

Churchill, Roosevelt, and Stalin at Yalta

England's exhaustion and Roosevelt's impending death useful in expanding his power.

Even as the Allies' leaders were departing Yalta, the beautiful German city of Dresden was incinerated by the first great aerial fire-bombing of the war. Perhaps 40,000 people were killed. The attack was intended to break the will of the German people and was immediately applied to Japan. There, on the night of March 9, 1945, three hundred American B29 Superfortresses dropped some 1,600 tons of napalm on Tokyo. Sixteen square miles of Tokyo were reduced to smoking ruin, as a rain of four-pound bags ignited and created a cauldron of fire.

Tokyo, Japan after the Fire Bombing

Perhaps 100,000 men, women, and children died; over a million became homeless. No greater loss had ever been inflicted by man upon any population in a single day in the whole of human history. Afterwards, except for the smoldering ruins, Tokyo had almost ceased to exist.

Despite the terrible losses, the firebombing failed to achieve its strategic intent. Japan continued to fight on ever more desperately, so dozens of other Japanese cities were firebombed in the next months. But even as Japanese cities were set afire, others were being spared to await a far worse fate.

Victory in Europe was declared just weeks after President Roosevelt's death. But the VE Celebration only allowed military planners to contemplate redeploying tired soldiers for an invasion of the Japanese home islands. Casualty estimates ran as high as a million. This frightful prospect was one they desperately sought to avoid.

President Truman, the former haberdasher from Missouri, took over the oval office upon the death of FDR. His sense of responsibility is remembered by a sign on his desk, "The buck stops here." He now faced the terrible choices surrounding the

Harry S Truman

impending invasion. They became worse when scientists tested the first Atomic Bomb at Alamogordo, New Mexico.

Little Boy was the name of the first bomb used in anger. The atomic blast over Hiroshima is estimated to have been the equivalent of 18,000 tons of TNT, i.e. 18 kilotons. Soon, this would be an almost trivial explosion. By 1952, the Hydrogen Bomb was developed. It uses an Atomic Bomb to start its ignition; as you would use a match to light a barbecue. The largest H-Bomb was tested by the Soviets. The *Tsar Bomb* was *only* 50 mega-tons – a compromise from a much larger one planned. Still, its *small* size was some ten times the total of all munitions used in WWII; its fireball gave third-degree burns to people 62 miles away from ground zero! Bombs four times larger were designed. They were intended to remove mountains – like Cheyenne, the headquarters of US' NORAD.

The Cold War

The United States emerged from the war relatively unscathed. Factories and mines stood able to transition their output to peace-time products. The only nation to possess the secret of the atom, it could have ruled the Earth. Instead, it launched a massive effort to rebuild friend and foe. But an age of peace did not ensue.

Winston Churchill declared that the Soviet Union dropped "an iron curtain" across Europe. The Cold War began when the USSR closed all land routes into Berlin. The allies responded by opening an air-corridor to the isolated city. Everything two million people needed to survive was delivered by plane: coal, clothes, food and even presents for the children. For ten months there was a touch-down every three minutes. Even the landing approaches were used to help the people below. As the aircraft entered their final descent, pilots dropped handkerchief-sized parachutes of candy to children. The wall around the city became a symbol of the competing political philosophies. When President Kennedy declared "Ich bin ein Berliner" – "I am a Berliner" he continued, "Freedom has many difficulties and democracy is not perfect, but we never had to put up a wall to keep our people in."

Half a world away, Chairman Mao Tse-tung took over China. His armies drove the Nationalists to the island of Formosa – now Taiwan. The *red tide* continued to Korea. Given the northern half of that peninsula, the USSR used it to launch an invasion of the South. But in one of History's great mistakes, the Soviet ambassador walked out of the United Nations' Security Council; so could not veto the – euphemistically called – *police action* where fifty three thousand UN troops, most US, died. The

Soviets provided covert support in the conflict, but China supplied men, who often attacked en masse. They suffered an estimated million soldiers killed from these tactics.

Seeing the End of Civilization

The war did not escalate to atomic warfare. This was a relief for all who feared the powers that had been unleashed by the Manhattan Project. It was close. General McArthur wanted to detonate multiple bombs on the China-Korea border. For this, among other things, he was relieved of duty by President Truman. Peace has yet to be declared in Korea – only an uneasy truce – and the war continues to add to its toll of casualties.

The worry about Communists bred paranoia. Senator Joseph McCarthy announced that he "had a list of members of the State Department who were communist sympathizers." The *Red Scare* unjustly ruined the lives of thousands. When a newly-elected President John Kennedy met the First Secretary of the Communist Party, Nikita Khrushchev, the meeting went badly. The First Secretary thought the young President "weak," and so tried to put nuclear missiles in Cuba to counter a similar U.S. deployment in Turkey. Again, the world came to the brink of an abyss.

John Kennedy (right)
Meeting Nikita Khrushchev

The horrors of trench warfare, first introduced in the American Civil War – and refined on the Western Front in World War I – had been eclipsed by the 60 million deaths of the Second World War. Yet, the devastation from firebombing of five-dozen Japanese cities is almost forgotten. It has been thrust from our collective minds because of the destruction of Hiroshima and Nagasaki by atomic bombs. At war's end, it was not the immediate joy of victory, nor sadness from the massive death and destruction that changed the world. These all paled when weighed against the contemplation of the instantaneous fury unleashed by the atom. With the A-Bomb's dawning, civilization – if not mankind itself – was in danger of ending in a flash.

But even as the world's arsenals had enough nuclear weapons stockpiled to kill every living creature several times, questions were asked about what could be even more horrible? The answer was: *a lot of things*. Nuclear war meant the destruction of cities, the end of civilization, and the eradication of humanity itself. But there remained the nightmare scenarios of the after-effects of any missile exchange, mutations from radiation or even a reversion to the stone-age following a *nuclear winter*. A debate began: Was it was better to die in the nuclear conflagration or to survive? Still, the superpowers continued to add to their nuclear arsenals adopting an aptly-named policy called Mutually Assured Destruction – MAD. This philosophy strove to keep the peace by ensuring that any attack by one superpower would guaranty the annihilation of both.

The world learned that once the atomic genie was out of the bottle, it could not be put back. The lesson was taught to children, who practiced huddling under their desks as a survival tactic. "Remember, children, duck and

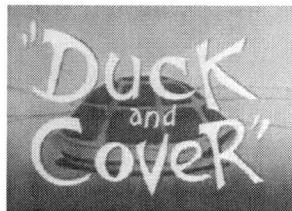

cover – and don't look at the blast through the windows." Homes throughout the county had fallout shelters built under their backyards. Efforts were made to make them chic. Office buildings had them in their lowest basements. Mountains were hollowed out and buildings were constructed within.

The cinemas were filled with movies about the malevolent results of radiation. Movies like *The Attack of the Fifty-foot Woman* and *Planet of the Apes* played to packed theaters. Movie Tone News added to the double-feature's entertainment showing open-air atom-bomb tests outside Las Vegas, Nevada. These tests were detonated like clockwork, once a month. Cows produced radioactive milk and gave birth to deformed calves. Women everywhere less feared the unseen impact upon their bodies than upon future children.

The Cold War was fought across the world and in the heavens. It had many manifestations, but for Americans, there was one singular event which served to highlight the stakes in what was certainly not a game. In 1957, the

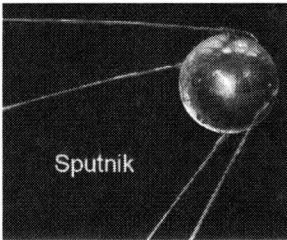
Sputnik

Soviet Union launched the first artificial space satellite, Sputnik - I. It orbited the globe every 96 minutes. This silver sphere measured less than two feet in diameter but its impact was far greater than its small size. It had antennas that continuously broadcast a 'beep' that was heard clearly by all. This pulse of radio noise symbolically conveyed three messages: "The USSR has taken the technological lead over the US;" "The USSR now owns space;" and the most frightening "We could drop an atomic bomb on the U.S. – and you cannot stop it."

Sputnik spawned *the space race*, and intensified the cold war. Monies were poured into science and the military; NASA was created. Key technologies were developed; perhaps most especially, digital computers. These quickly found their way into general use. One measure of the explosion of the information processing industry can be heard in a statement by Thomas Watson, the chairman of IBM, who in 1943 is alleged to have said: "I think there is a world market for maybe five computers." Today, their silicon successors number in the tens of billions!

And so the stage was set...

A New Kind of Network

A feature of American democracy is that the *research wealth* is distributed throughout the country, as each congressman secures contracts for their own constituents. The United States then, had to contend with the problem of facilitating communications between University, Industrial, and Military facilities that were often far from each other. Making the problem worse, each research center had different equipment collections. Their systems were being purchased from a computer industry that was birthing both new companies and new technologies daily. Researchers faced an explosion of technology as they also tried to protect the United States from very real thermonuclear ones.

Many different needs converged at the dawn of the Internet. There was the worry about cities disappearing; of national security; and protecting secrets from spies. There was also the need for a technical solution to the problem of linking the myriad different computing platforms to each other.

From many directions, a solution gradually evolved. The steps towards this solution can hide the description of the Internet's core that we would like to present. We are thus skipping the details, and going right to the logical heart of the Internet.

Over time, and with the participation of many brilliant minds, a communications model was developed which persists to this day. It came from Bell Laboratories, as well as from countless University and Corporate Researchers. The model was simple in concept, but with wide impact. The concept was to break any electronic message into pieces. Each *piece* could be sent independently to its intended destination. Each could be sent over a different route, or even at a different time. The pieces came to be called **packets** and a formal description of them was created, as well as rules for handling them. Each packet has two addresses: where they come from and their intended destination. Packets are numbered so they can be re-assembled at the receiving end.

The additional information was deemed to be the *envelope*, and as with a physical one, could be read by any intervening mail-carriers – or in this case, by computers charged with the task of passing the packets along toward their final destinations. Intermediate *nodes*, or communications computers, received a packet, looked at the destination address, and if it was not theirs, simply passed it on based on published *routing tables*.

This model guards the message and guaranties delivery. Missing sequence numbers are easy to spot and fix by re-sends. Messages are inherently more secure since an intercepted packet only contains a portion of the message. Operational problems with the network become less disruptive. If any intermediate node had a problem, an outage, or experiences congestion – even if it were destroyed – others act as replacement.   Packets can be *routed around* the problem. Traffic can be more easily managed, with heavily utilized routes *offloaded* to alternates.

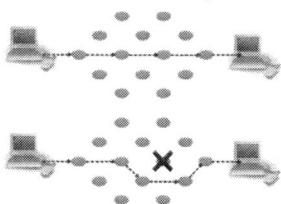

You now understand about the almost invisible things serving you on the web. They are so short-lived that their existence can be measured in millionths of a second; yet they simultaneously can last almost forever – in the form of *backups*. These packets are the building blocks of messages passing over a hidden infrastructure. So when you sit at your laptop at home, personal computer at work, or at a device that can now be located virtually anywhere, it is the packets' arrival you see. They bring things a little at a time – a picture of your best friend, a movie, or a *tweet* that a movie-star has just gotten drunk – by a mechanism whose genesis you now know.

Chapter 16 – THE INTERNET BECOMES...

You know that things are changing because of the Internet. It acts as a catalyst, a driver, and an enabler of change. Among its many capabilities, it seems to make distance disappear, or at least exhibits a casual disregard of distance. It provides access to an ocean of information through its uncountable links. The internet is used for communicating, coordinating, researching, teaching, and for entertaining. It links people to services, products, information, and most importantly to our brothers and sisters – humanity – around the globe. The Internet's uses seem limited only by human imagination both for good and not-so. Identity theft, online crime, and electronic harassment are an expensive and painful plague upon us all.

So what is this Internet? The last chapter likened it to the world's water system: an interconnected system of flowing information with many computers which store, provide, process, and control.

This chapter will show you what the Internet is. It will do so in a way that simplifies the complexity of what may be one of the world's most complicated systems – and there are many complicated systems out there. One of them is sitting in your chair right now – the human body. You will come to appreciate an important fundamental concept: the difference between the *Internet* and the *Web*. This will happen in just a few pages. We will now pick up the story from where we left off in the last chapter.

The Internet's Beginning

With the launch of Sputnik I, the United States was forced to recognize that the USSR could attack from space. The United States could not defend against or ignore this threat any more than it could quiet the maddening 'beeps' coming from above.

The United States had seen the extent of atomic warfare. Our doctors had treated many of its victims. Death from radiation poisoning was no longer a theory, but a terrible reality. Constant, ever-growing, above-ground (and hence, very public) detonations drove a multiple of related fears deep into the nations' psyche. These were augmented by other, cataclysmic fears, including new ones, like the prospect of a nuclear winter.

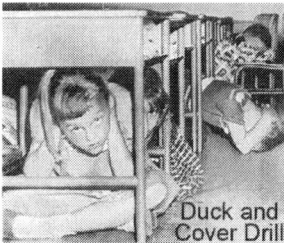
Duck and Cover Drill

Fear spawns action, and when an entire nation becomes frightened, it will do enormous things. So it was with the United States. Many initiatives were started.

One of them was suggested by two professors at MIT's Lincoln Laboratory, Jay Forrester and George Valley in the 1950's. They called for a defensive system to detect enemy bombers and guide interceptors to them. Called the Semi-Automatic Ground Environment (SAGE), it cost some $8-12 billion (in 1964 dollars). It was one of the first large computer networks and remained in continuous operation until 1983. The system had over two dozen computer centers with hundreds of radar sites to span the nation.

SAGE's IBM computers were the largest ever built. Each machine weighed over 250 tons and had 60,000 vacuum tubes. They consumed three million watts of power, occupied 20,000 square feet of floor-space, and were two stories high. A pair of identical computers was installed in windowless, blast-resistant concrete buildings. Each site was maintained by a team of 100.

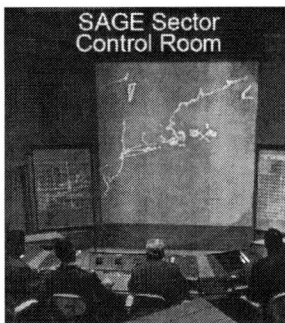

SAGE Sector Control Room

Beyond this one project, President Eisenhower institutionalized research and development for the Department of Defense. A new government agency was created to centralize this work. It was named the Advanced Research Projects Agency (ARPA). ARPA's first Director of Information Technology was a SAGE alumnus named J. C. R. Licklider. He had been a professor of psychology from MIT and was a pioneer in the field of human–computer interactions. Dr. Licklider's writings about an "Intergalactic Computer Network" describe much of what today comprises the Internet and they influenced many other related technologies.

J.C.R. Licklider

His ideas escaped the theoretical realm when a small, but growing problem asked to be solved. ARPA had been funding multiple research programs at various universities. A dedicated computer terminal was used to gain access to each school's computers. But, the number of terminals in ARPA's manager's offices began to grow as the number of schools increased. Worse, as you might guess, each system had a unique set of commands. This situation was becoming untenable both for the number of people who needed access to those systems, and for the forecast growth in the number of schools ARPA was planning to work with.

Then an event of global importance occurred. The Soviet Union's Premier, Nikita Khrushchev, tried to put nuclear-tipped missiles on the island of Cuba. U.S. President John F. Kennedy responded by using planes, ships, and submarines to blockade the island. This almost set *tomorrow* as the date when the horrors of nuclear war would arrive. The 1962 Cuban missile crisis was defused, thankfully. But the crisis showed that the U.S. military command and control system would not survive a nuclear exchange. Analysts determined that a critical vulnerability existed in the underlying network technology that was used – it was *circuit-switched.* That meant that a physical line had to be connected from here to there. A nuclear exchange could shut down the nation by severing any one of these links.

Work was begun on a decentralized system that could continue to work even if large parts of the network were destroyed. What the engineers designed would eventually also solve the problem of the managers' multiple terminals.

As the military's R & D nerve-center, ARPA issued a *request for proposal* for firms to compete for the right to design and build critical elements of the new system. The company, Bolt, Beranek and Newman (now BBN

Technologies) was chosen to build the device which would act as the *brains* of the network. They called it an *Interface Message Processor.* Today, we know it as a *router* (more about that later). The first IMPs linked three university computer systems: Stanford, the University of

California at Santa Barbara and at Los Angeles, and the University of Utah. These four sites all joined a new, *high-speed* network: ARPANET. It worked at 5,000 characters per second (50 kbs). On October 29th, 1969, the first message was sent from UCLA by a student programmer. During the attempt, the system crashed, but the first two letters of the message – "login" – were successfully transmitted.

Initially ARPANET was used to transfer files. That function quickly expanded. The first networked e-mail was sent in 1971 by Ray Tomlinson – who chose the now-famous "@" symbol used in email addresses. Two years later, e-mail comprised 75% of all network traffic. Four decades later, *spam*, i.e. unsolicited e-mail, accounts for billions of deliveries each day – by far, the largest e-mail use of the system. Spam has become such a problem that many are ending their use of e-mail. Voice transmission capabilities were also quickly added, but the quality was unsatisfactory for many years (so, too, was real-time video after that).

ARPANET was an instant success. The benefits were clear. The new technology called *Packet-Switching* allowed any device to reach any other through any available connection. Response time and reliability were acceptable and you did not have to break the bank to get on it. The system began to grow exponentially: from one new university per quarter to a new connection each day. The initial four became two hundred. Then the era of the Internet began, with its growth through the thousands and millions to now, billions of links.

The Internet Grows

The problem which ARPANET solved was a common one. Many other computer professionals saw what had been done, and built their own packet-switching networks. This, of course, led to another problem: How could each of the new networks communicate with the others? It took just four years for ARPA to begin a new research effort to try and solve this. It was called the *Inter-netting Project*.

We are reminded of what they did, even if who did the work is forgotten, by the oft-seen letters: ***TCP / IP***. That ungainly acronym stands for *Transmission Control Protocol / Internet Protocol*. The *TCP* part refers to the rules used to improve and regulate how information is transmitted over the network. These protocols were designed to be layered, or used on top of the existing rules used to control the still-immature Internet – the Internet Protocol (IP).

Together, individual networks could interconnect seamlessly thereby creating one vast network. Originally, users would *address* their messages by way of a numeric address. By 1984, using numbers (e.g. 155.136.232.062) became unwieldy, so they were replaced by the current system which uses names (e.g. www.google.com).

But someone or something needed to keep track of the names so that they were unique and so that the name could be converted to a number which the network still ultimately required. Initially, all internet addresses were contained in a single file named: *etc/hosts.txt* which had both name and equivalent number. This has since been replaced by the *Internet Registry* organization which allocates system identifiers and maintains the *Domain Name System* (DNS). So, when you type in a name, it is fed to a one of many DNS servers which converts it to a number.

Demand for Internet services continued to explode and it was decided that ARPA's mission was not one of operational support. ARPANET was decommissioned in 1990, after the U.S. National Science Foundation deployed NSFNET as a backbone for the Internet. Other organizations have since added their own resources. Today, the Internet runs on multiple, decentralized backbones: NASA, the U.S. Department of Energy, and similarly, many entities around the world.

In 1993, the U.S. Congress passed a law (which Senator Al Gore famously co-sponsored) to allow private companies to provide *Network Access Points*. This was done by auction and four companies were the winners. This is the clear beginning of the commercialization of the Internet. It took the Internet out of Government hands and made it available to private users. This has fostered many interesting new uses, and some not-so. You could argue that the true *winner* of that auction is the entire human race!

You might ask how one *reaches* the Internet. One way of thinking about this is the term: *the last mile*. For most of the public, this last mile is the link from where you are to the local communications carrier – yesterday's telephone company. This was once a pair of copper wires into each home. These could carry only a few hundred characters per second; now the technology enables them to carry multiple millions. *Wireless* technologies are also part of this *last mile*, enabling access from virtually anywhere.

There are many, many organizations today which maintain the physical hardware that makes the Internet run. This hardware includes computer servers, switches, hubs, routers, and cabling. The cabling that carries the Internet takes many forms: copper wire; fiber-optic cable; coaxial cable; and even wireless and satellite transmissions. When you want to connect to the Internet, you must first arrange with an *Internet Service Provider* (ISP) to allow you access. Usually, this means you have to pay for the access typically to a phone, cable, or satellite company. This company will assign you your very own address to use on the Internet and provide you with a physical (or wireless) connection.

A *modem* (short for MOdulating/DEModulating device) is often used to convert your computer's network signal into something the ISP can use. A *router* may also be used. It literally acts like a traffic cop as it allows any user to link to multiple computers through a single connection.

There are other technologies, too, and more to come, still. Business users have their own version of these access technologies with the very largest firms providing sophisticated access to their own, internal Internets – sometimes referred to as *Intranets* – along with subsequent access to other networks.

Two intriguing new uses of the Internet are just in their infancy. In the first, NASA is developing ways to

International Space Station

extend the Internet into space. When colonies are eventually settled on the Moon and Mars (and beyond?) and as more people live in orbit, those pioneers will need a method of permanently connecting to the Internet. So a way needs to be created to extend the Internet's *backbone* into our Solar System. Perhaps, someday, you might type a web address with a ".moon" in its name!

In the second, today, *hot spots* exist in various places which allow a user to wirelessly and automatically connect to the Internet when in range of the signal. As more of these hot spots are put online, a user will have the ability to continually have wireless access to the net. Eventually, this will eliminate the need for all wired connections and will create a permanent *cloud* of information making the Internet as pervasive and ubiquitous as the air we breathe.

If you consider the beginnings of the Internet, it remains true to its roots. What we call the Internet is a collection of interconnected, very large, high-speed networks. These have been built by both commercial and government entities. Some encircle the globe, others serve narrowly defined areas. It exists to provide access from most-anywhere to most-anything.

No one owns the Internet. There is no single point of control of its operations – no central management. Nowhere does all the traffic pass through a single location. Indeed, a guiding principle was to have a network that could survive any disaster so there is no *single point of failure*. The growth of the Internet continues unabatedly by all measures: computers, users, services, information, or traffic.

The Web Arrives

The *Internet* is related to, but different from the *Web*. Understanding this is important to your understanding of what is surrounding you. Thus far, you have read about the creation, evolution, and expansion of the Internet. It is a physical network of hardware and software; it is the medium over which information flows. The Internet has many uses: e-mail., location/directions, *tweets*, streaming audio and video, etc.

But, there is one use that defines the Web:

...to interconnect any part of the knowledge of mankind to any other, no matter where either is located.

This idea, or *mission statement*, first appeared in a 1945 magazine article by Dr. Vannevar Bush. Dr. Bush was appointed by President Roosevelt to head the Office of Scientific Research and Development, the organization coordinating weapons development research for the Second World War – it would later became ARPA.   He was effectively the first Presidential Science Advisor and one of the primary organizers of the atom-bomb-building Manhattan Project.

In one of his many articles he described a "memory-extension box," the "Memex:"

"...a device in which an individual stores all his books, records, and communications...which is mechanized so that it may be consulted with exceeding speed and flexibility. It is an enlarged intimate supplement to his memory."

His vision was limited due to the technology available at the time.   The article described a photo-electrical machine linking documents stored on microfilm.   His words described a *Web* – just not today's. It would take almost exactly two decades for the technology to catch up with the vision, which remains one of the core ideas of the Web.

In 1963, Ted Nelson, a graduate student at Harvard, doing research in word processing called linking information, **Hypertext**. What this means is ordinary text augmented by active links to other data. Ted began the first project in this space, one that still continues: the *Xanadu Project*. Many people, schools, and then companies entered the field. The first working system was built at Brown University in 1967. Their *Hypertext Editing System* was later used to create documentation for the Apollo space program.

All these efforts extended the early, rudimentary ability to jump between documents. But they were limited in linking to anything other than local information. This was because of the limitations of connecting geographically and technologically diverse computers, as described earlier. More complex Hypertext development continued. One project was by Tim Berners-Lee, a researcher at CERN (the European organization for nuclear research). He wrote a program which allowed information links to be made across computers. This was another of the core building blocks of the Web.

Tim Berners-Lee

Three more of Berners-Lee's programs leveraged advances in the Internet's infrastructure: the *browser*, the *Hypertext Transfer Protocol* (HTTP), and the *Hypertext Markup Language* (HTML). A *browser* is a computer program that you use to access the Web. Popular browsers include Microsoft's Internet Explorer, Mozilla's Firefox, and

Example of HTML

```
<!DOCTYPE HTML>
<HTML>
  <HEAD>
    <TITLE>Hello HTML</TITLE>
  </HEAD>
  <BODY>
    <P>Hello World!</P>
  </BODY>
</HTML>
```

Google's Chrome. HTTP is the set of rules used to send web pages over the Internet. HTML is the computer language that is used to create a web page.

Let's put all of this together. When you go to a web site by entering its address into your *browser*, the *DNS server* converts the name into a numerical address and sends your request to the right web server. That web server responds by sending the requested web page. That transfer of data uses the rules of *HTTP* to communicate. The web page is sent to your browser in *HTML* format. Your browser then converts that language into a viewable page for you to see and interact with.

Berners-Lee's work was more an indication of how to solve a problem than it was a fully functional solution. He offered them to the Internet community of developers for comment, development, and expansion. The *openness* of this process was, and is, a critical element in achieving their wide acceptance.

You might ask: If the Web is how I normally interact with the Internet, is there anything other than the web on the Internet? Yes, there are dozens of other protocols (rules) that are used on the Internet to communicate information between computers. They have names like POP (for email), FTP (for transferring files), SCTP (for streaming video and audio), and many others. The details of these other protocols are not important for two reasons: They are secondary in importance to TCP, HTTP and the Web; and many are becoming obsolete – subsumed by the currently-omnipotent Web.

Not mentioned until now, but of critical importance, is that all of this was taking place in the *personal computer* era, when having a computer in the home was becoming natural – indeed, mandatory. Together, these hardware, software, and communications intersections made the Internet accessible to those who embrace computers and those who shun them. They allowed the enormous mass of information stored in the world's information systems to become accessible to all via the Web. Its immodest goal: the collection and dissemination of the sum-total of human knowledge.

Now, you understand a bit about the Internet providing communications to a multitude of systems and the Web riding atop with its never-ending chains of information. Each represents capabilities which have never before existed and that are changing our world: governmentally, commercially, socially, personally, and even religiously. Understanding these fundamentals adds to your ability to succeed. There is a very deep pool of additional information you can dive into. It is easy to find and to access.

Information, Information

We keep using the word "information." This casual use hides an important-to-you fundamental. Today, the amount of available information is vastly larger than ever before – and the word *vastly* is woefully inadequate to describe the explosion in information that has occurred. The amount of it is expanding continually and exponentially!

When the first copy of the Gutenberg Bible was printed, it represented a quantum change from expensive, individually hand-written copies of books for the few, to mass-produced ones that could be acquired by the many. In the over 500 years since the arrival of movable type printing, books have gone from being printed on paper to not being printed at all. The latter state, being *virtual*, removes any physical burden imposed by books' historical form. They can now be copied, transmitted, searched, or whatever, virtually instantaneously. A *book* is no longer simply a *book*.

The change to the information world is far greater than what has happened to that of books. They only represent a small percentage of what is available. Even the categories of information now include many which never existed before. Besides the text of books, there are virtual magazines, articles, blogs, forums, and *tweets*. But text is just the tip of the information iceberg. Numbers of all sorts are to be found, grouped, or subdivided; all graphed in multiple dimensions. But the ocean gets deeper still with sound and image both stored and real-time. The list of data contains coordinates and maps of friends and of a thousand other types including information about information – called metadata. How many *clicks* were there today; how often did your cursor hover over a link on your screen without actually clicking; how many made purchases from Wal-Mart or Amazon?

Entirely new information sources have been born. One astronomy project is in New Mexico. It is called the Sloan Digital Sky Survey. It was begun in the year 2000 and its telescope collected more data about the sky above us in the first few weeks of its operation than had been amassed in the whole of human history. When its successor comes on-line, every five days it will acquire 10 years' worth of SDSS data! There are many such information-creating projects being built. CERN's Geneva laboratory has the Large Hadron Collider. It generates 40 Terabytes of new information – every second. The size of that number will be clear in a few paragraphs.

One character on this page is called, in technical terms, a byte, with a typical half-page of text containing about a thousand of them, a Kilobyte (kB). Five hundred pages contain about a million characters, or a Megabyte (MB). The complete works of Shakespeare measures about 5MBs. A billion characters are called a Gigabyte (GB), and would occupy about 500,000 pages. This is about the same storage needed for a single, 2-hour movie – It would seem that the axiom "A picture is worth a thousand words" holds true. You will notice that each division is 1,000 times larger than the last (actually 1,024 times larger – as the divisions reflect powers of two: 2^{10}, 2^{20}, 2^{30}).

Next is the Terabyte (TB), 2^{40}. The entire Library of Congress occupies about 20 of them, which is why CERN creating 40 TB per second is so impressive! But the pool of information is far, far larger than that. The total information that Google processes every hour is about 5 Petabytes 5×2^{50}. This fact will be true for only a very short time as it will certainly grow, but it does put the information *explosion* that is happening into perspective.

The Exabyte is 2^{60}, but the amount of information available today is estimated to be a thousand times larger, more than a Zettabyte's worth (2^{70}). Will the amount of data ever touch the Yottabyte (2^{80})? It seems the answer to that is yes, with only this question remaining: "How soon?" As an aside, how does that number compare to how many stars there are in the Universe (estimated to be 10^{21} – 1,000,000,000,000,000,000,000)? The last question is asked with a smile – the numbers are so big that it is amusing to note that it is hard to know which is larger.

The fundamental point remains: The amount of information astounds, is growing, and that knowing of its existence allows you to think differently about the world.

Dot-com Bubble and Afterwards

This chapter ends with a tale about the dollars and cents in your pocket – specifically about the commercialization of the Internet. From the beginning, the Internet blazed a new frontier – a virtual place where new business products and services are offered. It is easy to enter, but competition is found there, too. In the early days (as far back as the end of the second millennium), ideas were drafted and investors enticed. Though it seemed many concepts were drawn on napkins during lunch; monies were attracted and spent. Companies quickly learned that putting an "e-" before their name, followed by a ".com", instantly made them more valuable. Sometimes they only changed their names. Norris Communications became "e.Digital" and its stock soared from $.06 a share to $24.50 in 12 months. Later, as you might expect, it fell all the way back, but those who bought at the peak were badly injured financially.

Firms' stock-market valuations lost the connection between the price of their stock and their earnings (P/E). Many of the new companies tried to build market share by offering their products at a loss. Some of the amounts of money lost this way were impressive: "Boo.com" spent $188 million in just 6 months before going bankrupt. "E-Toys.com" raised $166 million; spent it all; then bankruptcy found its stock down from $84 to $.09.

Huge fortunes were made and lost during this period. Later, the question became "How did this happen?" "TheGlobe.com" was begun by two college students. They initially received $15,000 to buy a computer. Twenty-four months later investors gave them $20 million. A year later they offered stock to the public. On the first day shares went from $9.00 to $97.00. Their startup became valued at almost a billion dollars; each of the two young founders became Internet hundred-millionaires. The company never turned a profit and its flagship site closed soon after the crash. Another tale is the company famous for having become a very popular Internet destination. The amazing part of the story is that "Geocities.com" went from birth to death never having made a penny of profit and yet was valued, indeed purchased, for $3.57 billion. We wonder if there was promotion of the guilty and punishment for the innocent for that buy?

The *Bubble* reached its high-point on March 10, 2000, when the NASDAQ hit over 5,000; within a year, that would be halved, wiping out some $5 trillion of investor wealth.

There are two lessons from these years. First, is that there are cycles where millions act as one, no matter how irrationally.

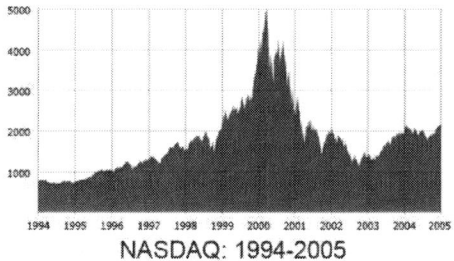

NASDAQ: 1994-2005

We later devote a chapter to this topic. Second, is that all the excesses and bad smells of the Internet Bubble could be considered the products of the birth of something new.

The Internet and the Web have grown, and continue to do so by any measurement or view-point. The many dot-com learning lessons – at least something came from its failures – pale, however, beside the successes of that era. Much was spawned that continues; much is continuing to be spawned.

Today we have several ways to access the web. The information available to us can be presented as a list through the many *search-engines* like Google, Yahoo, and Bing. Our modes of communications have been changed: email, tweets, instant messages, Skype, etc. We get to see pictures and videos taken by virtually anyone, anywhere – in real time. People's locations, schedules and friends are instantly accessible – their very thoughts, too – almost seen in their blog postings.

How business is transacted – middlemen, geography, inventory – are all different thanks to that era. Entertainment has changed in ways that were previously unimaginable. The way that the music and movie industries market and distribute their products is being completely transformed – and what about the images and sounds you see and hear! Travel has changed, with $360°$ views of any of the world's locations now available from a device you use while somewhere else – or just around the block. You can always know where you are and how to get where you are going. But there are still risks, ones that never existed before: electronic worms, viruses, and even having your identity stolen.

Being aware of the Internet and of the Web is vital. They have changed the world and are doing so ever-more broadly. We have given you an introduction that we believe will serve you in good stead and one that you will extend to your benefit

Chapter 17 – YOU CAN MAKE MISTAKES

This book has presented a wide variety of topics for your edification, entertainment, and contemplation.

"Jenny" Stamp Error - 1918

They have all been focused on helping you succeed – whether through new skills or information. For the latter, know that recognizing reality as clearly as possible is essential for moving forward successfully.

But no one is perfect and usually, all of the information needed is not available to you. Mistakes will be made. Alexander Pope may have said it best: "To err is human." Usually, mistakes are categorized as being either ones of *commission* or ones of *omission*. The former resulting from those things we did and the latter from things which we did not do. There are another two perspectives from which they can be viewed.

MS Costa Concordia, Italy - 2012

The first of these is to note that there are those who never make mistakes. You can identify them because they never *do* anything – so they never screw up. We believe that those who *do*, make mistakes; we hope that you will be among them because you have chosen to *do*. In this spirit, let us remember a friend of ours who, when coming into a new job, told his team "make lots of mistakes, but make them early."

I-35 Bridge Collapse - 2007

Of course, you want to minimize your mistakes; you will not benefit from making too many of them or from making worse ones. The simple act of moving forward exposes you to the chance of error, but even when that chance becomes reality, there can be benefits. Remember Thomas Edison failed in thousands of ways as he moved toward the creation of the electric light; the expert is often the person who has experienced the most mistakes.

Once you recognize that mistakes will happen, your task must be to learn from your mistakes. To paraphrase George Santayana: "Those who fail to learn from their mistakes are destined to repeat them." A related sentiment attributed to Benjamin Franklin defines insanity as "doing the same thing over and over and expecting different results." Learning why and how your mistake was made and then taking steps to prevent it from recurring can only make you better. Certainly, Edison learned from his many mistakes. He did not throw up his hands and declare his efforts all for nothing. He collected the data from his failures and studied them. Then he tried again.

First Mid-Air Collision, Milan, Italy - 1910

The second perspective is that there is a special class of mistakes in which reality is denied. This happens all the time. The Scottish historian Charles Mackay wrote a book on it called *Extraordinary Popular Delusions and the Madness of Crowds*. There he detailed national follies like England's South Sea Bubble and Holland's Tulip Frenzy. He wrote: "Men, it has been well said, think in herds; it will be seen that they go mad in herds, while they only recover their senses slowly, one by one." A more recent, but eerily similar set of events occurred in the infamous *dot-com bubble* (discussed in a previous chapter) that caused a financial melt-down at the dawn of the millennium.

Charles Mackay

These well-known events illustrate how mindlessly traveling in a herd (aka the herd mentality) can be a recipe for disaster. You must always keep your wits about you and question the perceived logic of the situation. Never allow yourself to be lulled into a false sense of safety just because "everyone else is doing it."

Tacoma Narrows Bridge Collapse 1940

This does not imply that knowing is easy, or that information is ever complete. Knowledge is shaped by many factors, but here we highlight two, briefly: bias, and perspective. Bias restricts information to a subset that has been predetermined. Sometimes, biases have a basis in fact and experience. In the absence of information, they become the basis for decisions. However, you should never base a decision knowingly on a biased basis if there is contradicting information available. In so doing, you may well be discarding much of value because it simply *cannot be*, while more is imputed because it *has to be*. Never limit the scope of your understanding of a situation; always be ready to accept the unexpected.

Perspective, on the other hand, adds to the data by comparing it to its surroundings. Getting the *big picture* can make even imperfect knowledge better.

What follows are a few examples to illustrate how very easy it is to make mistakes. Sometimes these mistakes are made by many. The consequences of doing so can be...well, you'll see.

Misunderstanding Reality

Everyone knows what a Brontosaurus is (or was). You can probably, easily draw a picture of one or would recognize one if you saw someone else's drawing. There is just one tiny thing:

There is no such animal nor has there ever been such a one!

The story of how we today *know* of the Brontosaurus illustrates how truth can become distorted and yet enters into the realm of *the well-known*.

In the late 1800's, Yale's great paleontologist, Dr. Othniel Marsh, declared a newly-uncovered juvenile skeleton to be a new type of dinosaur. Though incomplete, there was enough for him to name it *Apatosaurus*. Two years later, a bluff in Wyoming revealed what it had long hidden, the largest skeleton in the world. It dwarfed all other dinosaur finds and was virtually complete except for its head and feet. After a detailed examination, Dr. Marsh gave it the wonderfully evocative name *Brontosaurus*, meaning *Thunder-lizard*.

Yale's Peabody Museum decided to put it on display, mounted upright for the first time ever. This allowed the

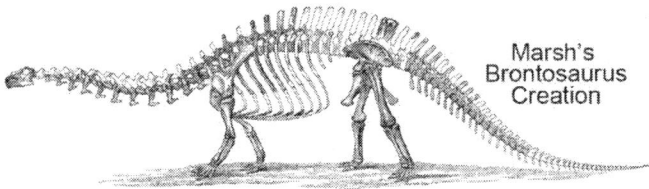

Marsh's
Brontosaurus
Creation

public to truly appreciate the enormity of these long-dead animals. The skeleton can still be seen there, with a head in place, one they modeled after another dinosaur, the *Camarasaurus*. The display captured the public's imagination and caused a sensation that is remembered till today.

Unfortunately, Dr. Marsh and the Peabody Museum were mistaken. The larger skeleton dubbed Brontosaurus was actually an adult Apatosaurus. Adding a model of a Camarasaurus head created a fictitious dinosaur. While the exhibit took place in 1905, the measure of how far it exceeded the Museum's expectations can be seen in the fact that a plaster head atop the body of an adult Apatosaurus is still remembered as a Brontosaurus. The illusion became so engrained that some field excavators ignored fossil skulls that they found *knowing* them to be *wrong*.

Here, the consequences of not recognizing that the child skeleton was the same dinosaur as the adult are only amusing – to those who know; for all the rest...watch out for the Brontosaurus!

Apatosaurus

*   *   *   *   *

Chancellorsville, a battle during the American Civil War, is considered General Robert E. Lee's greatest strategic triumph. The armies that fought were so unequal in size that the outcome of the battle seemed foreordained. The Union Army was more than double the Confederate.

Hostilities began with General Lee splitting his army; 10,000 men were left behind as a screen to prevent his being attacked from two directions at once. He then split his army again, sending half on a 14 mile march around the Union line – a maneuver known as a flanking movement. This left Lee with a greatly depleted force of only 25,000 men to face the Union army of over 130,000 men. The Union Army's commander, General Joseph Hooker, could clearly see the troops leaving the field of battle. They were also seen when they reappeared before the far right flank of the Union line. Lookouts posted high in the trees saw the impending attack on the end of the line. A runner was dispatched to headquarters.

Robert E. Lee

Joseph Hooker

Unfortunately for the Union Army that day, General Hooker *knew* that General Lee was retreating. He felt that the lookouts were simply excited and did not understand what they were seeing. In retrospect, his judgment of Lee's courage would better have been measured against the record of General Lee and his Army of Northern Virginia – they never ran.

The length of the march to the Union flank had caused the attack to be launched as evening fell. Confederate General Thomas "Stonewall" Jackson led the flanking movement. His troops attacked the Union flank and crushed the opposing force, driving them in chaos backwards. Eventually the numerically superior Federal troops were able to form defensive positions. They even counterattacked. Darkness would add to both sides' disorganization and end the fighting though Jackson tried to press his advantage and continue the attack.

Due to General Lee's audacity, General Jackson's tenacity, but mostly to General Hooker's mistake, the victory belonged to the Confederates. There were over 30,000 casualties that day with the bulk of them on the Union side. Worse, however, was that Hooker's biased judgment of Lee's character not only was the cause of his army's defeat, but it allowed the American Civil War to continue for two more, ever-bloody years.

         *   *   *   *   *

The Great Battleship Race began with another battle of the American Civil War, a draw between the USS Monitor and the CSS Virginia (formerly the USS Merrimack). This was the first time that ironclad warships had ever fought each other. On that day, every wooden fighting ship in the world became instantly obsolete.

Battle of Hampton Roads: USS Monitor vs CSS Virginia

Seafaring nations began to compete in building iron battleships. Fifty years later these finally came to the test in the Russo-Japanese War. This began when Japan objected to Russia's leasing the Chinese city of Lushun, aka Port Arthur, a year-round, ice-free Pacific prize. The Japanese launched a siege from their occupied Manchurian bases and were eventually able to sink the entire Russian far-east fleet by shelling it as it sheltered in the harbor.

In response, the Russians dispatched their main battle fleet almost half way around the world. The line of Russian battleships arrived in the waters between Korea and Japan – the straits of Tsushima – and encountered a perpendicular line of new Japanese battleships. The two fleets together joined to form a capital 'T,' the perfect naval battle formation – at least for one side. In this formation all the Japanese guns (four big guns per ship) could fire upon the Russian battleships simultaneously, while only the two fore guns of the lead Russian ship could fire in return. The Russians tried to turn, but with their bottoms badly fouled and their speed degraded their efforts were ineffective, and nearly the entire fleet was destroyed.

British observers watched and assessed the battle. Their admirals then ordered the construction of a new ship whose very name is remembered as a symbol of sea dominance. The HMS Dreadnought, launched in 1906, was armed with ten 12-inch guns. It was also faster and more heavily armored than the typical battleship of the day. Weighing in at 18,000 tons, on the day it was launched, it obsolesced every warship in the

HMS Dreadnought

entire world.

Other navies compared their fleets to the English and determined that they trailed the British by only one ship. Any navy who could launch a single bigger battleship could dominate the world. The race to build bigger battleships continued another 30 years. It culminated in Japan's 1937 launch of the Yamato. This behemoth, along with her sister ship, Musashi, weighed 72,000 tons and was armed with nine 18.1 inch main turret guns and a dozen six inch guns. It was sunk by aircraft on its final, suicide attack against the entire U.S. fleet outside of Okinawa in the waning weeks of the war. A dozen torpedo hits against the port side failed to capsize the ship. The many 500 pound bomb hits also failed to sink her. She would die only after her main magazine exploded in the largest conventional explosion to have ever been seen at sea.

Yet the mistake that you will now learn about took place almost 25 years before the Yamato's end. In the midst of the great battleship race, U.S. Brigadier General Billy Mitchell argued that the naval battleship had lost its dominance to the virtually brand new, almost trivially weak, Air Force. More than that, he demonstrated the fact. His airplane squadron of WWI bi-planes easily sank a fleet of captured German WWI battleships. This was a non-arguable

General Billy Mitchell

demonstration of air power, yet the Joint Board of the Army and the Navy promptly declared: "The battleship is still the backbone of the fleet." General Mitchell was court-martialed for his efforts.

This episode shows how hard it is for military strategists to adapt to changing times and technologies. It also illustrates how a prophet is both perceived as having no honor in his own country and is particularly unwelcome in the military. General Mitchell predicted Japan's use of airpower against *sitting ducks* like the entire Pacific Fleet at Pearl Harbor. His vision also included high altitude bombers, parachutists, and much more. By the end of WWII, the battleship was an anachronism. Today, no country maintains active battleships.

The cost of the mistake was less to Billy – his career ended – but to the United States being so much less prepared for the Second World War than it could have been otherwise. The cost may also be measured in the millions who died in the extra years of war that the lack of preparation caused.

*   *   *   *   *

Living in Stalin's Russia was to live under threat of execution. Anyone even suspected of offering opposition to his authority could find themselves in a gulag. So, when Stalin ordered his architects to create a gigantic building for him across the street from Moscow's Kremlin, it must have been both pleasing and terrifying to them.

Joseph Stalin

It is a massive structure, like many of its ilk. However, it is unlike the others in an interesting fashion. The left half of the building does not resemble the right. It is almost as if the whole was constructed from disparate plans – which, actually turns out to be the truth.

The architects had drawn two sets of plans intending to offer Stalin a choice. However, when the plans were presented to him, they were not in the room. Not realizing that a choice was being offered to him, Stalin initialed both sets. The architects thus were faced with a dilemma: whether or not to tell the dictator he'd made a mistake. The solution was to keep quiet and build the only building in the city so constructed – and hope that Stalin would not notice.

"Power tends to corrupt and absolute power corrupts absolutely" is a truism by John Dalberg-Acton and is related to an idea attributed to Edmund Burke: "the only condition necessary for evil to succeed is for good men to stay silent." How many times and places have those in power made mistakes which went uncorrected?

Now you are not a tyrant or dictator, but you must ensure that others should always feel able to come to you with problems and issues. An open door policy is always preferred and an atmosphere of understanding and professionalism will prevent small mistakes from becoming big ones.

*   *   *   *   *

Traveling to Mars has been a dream of many on this planet for millennia. This dream may well come to fruition in only a matter of years. In preparation for an eventual manned expedition to that mysterious orb, NASA and other space agencies have been sending a series of robotic spacecraft to Mars to probe its secrets.

One such mission was the *Mars Climate Orbiter* launched in 1998. Its task was to orbit Mars and uncover details on its climate and atmosphere, and on changes that occur on its surface. The launch and long trip to Mars proceeded uneventfully.

Mars

Nearly a year after launch, the orbiter finally reached the red planet. Firing its thrusters, it was scheduled to swing around the planet and enter permanent orbit. Flight controllers on the ground issued the appropriate orders to the spacecraft so that the engines would fire with exactly the correct intensity and for the prescribed amount of time. The spacecraft flew behind the planet and into a planned radio blackout. The flight controllers waited for it to reappear from behind the planet to reacquire the radio signal. They never heard from the spacecraft again!

After an investigation, it was determined that the wrong instructions were sent to the orbiter. When the engineers and scientists planned the mission, they intended to send the spacecraft the amount of force that the engines would use when firing. The spacecraft expected this data to be in the form of a metric unit called *Newtons* (named after that great scientist). Unfortunately, the flight controllers didn't know this and assumed that they would be communicating this data to the spacecraft in the Imperial manner which is called *pounds-force*. So the controllers and the spacecraft were effectively communicating in different languages and didn't know it.

Mars Climate Orbiter

This is analogous to telling someone to travel 10 miles when they thought you meant 10 kilometers.

The controllers *knew* they were using the correct *language*. It never occurred to them to question their own actions. The result? A $350 million pile of debris is strewn somewhere across Mars' surface.

As with all the other chapters in this work, you have seen some of the very many examples which strive to be both entertaining and to remind you that "mistakes happen – deal with them." Mistakes have always been used to entertain. Some of those stories are counted among the world's greatest literature, e.g. Shakespeare's *Romeo and Juliet*.

Equally important, while keeping the certainty of mistakes in mind, your fear of them should be lessened; you might feel more confident and thus make more of them, more often. It is a fine line between making too many and making too few. Anticipating, recognizing, even welcoming mistakes can be a vital element in reaping their help and benefits.

Chapter 18 – YOU ARE SMART

One of the greatest obstacles to success can be a mistaken conviction that you are, if not exactly stupid, just not that smart. Perhaps you were made fun of when little or your grades were less than great in school. You may have been overweight or not a good athlete. It could be that people have belittled your job or the career you've had. There are many blows to our psyche that have to be absorbed and the damage to one's sense of self-confidence can be severe. Life can become a rut that you fall into and follow endlessly. Rare are the flashes of genius – or of luck – that lift you up onto a different path.

You can overcome this. The truth is that you are smarter than you give yourself credit for. This is an easy statement to make, because there is no question of it. This is true of everyone – even of those who might be classified as *mentally challenged*. Some of these people are spectacular living proof that everyone is smart in some way. Those with universally recognized areas of brilliance are even known by a popular, if unflattering term. They are called *savants* (formerly idiot-savant) and they are examples both of the wonders of the mind and of an individual's uniqueness (remember the movie *Rain Man*?).

What is true for mental disabilities is valid, too, for physical ones. Everyone knows that when one sense is lost – the ability to see, for example – the brain can adapt by making the other senses more acute. These two illustrations highlight what is too often misunderstood or forgotten: People differ in the areas in which they are smart. What is easy for one may not be for another. This is one reason why there is power in diversity. But society favors certain abilities and talents over others. If you do not possess the favored abilities, you may be considered slow or untalented but your talents may simply be elsewhere.

You, however, might lack ready proof of this. Here, then, is something that will make others say "Wow!" It is intended to be proof, if you ever need it, of your mind's abilities for you to use as required. This is just one of the many such things that you know but are not aware of.

When the question "Who is the smartest person who ever lived?" is asked, Albert Einstein's name is usually atop the list. The fame he achieved in life remains with us. He sits high in the pantheon of the brilliant minds of history in popular culture – and for good reason.

But most people do not understand what Dr. Einstein is famous for. Was it something to do with the atomic bomb? That Einstein forever changed the way we view our Universe is true, but not helpful in answering the question.

Before Einstein, everyone understood that we lived surrounded by something called *space*, this included: the ground we stand on, the air above, and the vast beyond. Travel in this Universe was a matter of a journey in a straight line from here to there. *Time* was an intangible, immutable thing that flowed by and measured

the passage of our lives. At one time, there were mysteries like why the Moon did not fall to Earth. Sir Isaac Newton then saw an apple fall. This event provided him with an insight on how gravity affected everything. He then developed a more complete explanation of the world around us. But there were still open questions.

A young Albert had a different experience leading to his own *Eureka!* moment. He took a trolley ride and looked back at a clock-tower. Suddenly, he realized the real nature of the Universe – a nature no one before him had fully grasped. He discovered **space-time**. This is a radically different definition of everything around us. He described a fantastic universe that has since been experimentally proven to be as he predicted – but left certain unanswered questions for others to ponder. Science is like that.

We propose that you become one of the people who can prove the existence of *space-time*. To make it very easy, we will give you a mystery. You don't have to solve it – Einstein did that – all you have to do is be able to show that the solution is true. Sir Arthur Conan Doyle's Sherlock Holmes put it this way: "When you eliminate the impossible, whatever remains, no matter how improbable, must be the truth." Space-time is very improbable, it is non-intuitive, but proving it to be real turns out to be easy. You just do not know how to do so yet. You will, though, in just a few pages.

Here's the setting for our mystery. You and your identical twin, Dale, are sitting on a couch watching TV. Suddenly, Dale decides to visit a distant star and goes outside to where your spaceship is parked. Dale climbs in and takes off. It flies at almost the speed of light (don't worry about the time it takes to speed up and slow down). Eventually the ship reaches the distant star.

Dale's wristwatch shows that it took exactly one year to get there. Dale enjoys looking at the star for an hour, then comes back home – which, by his watch, takes another year – and sits back down on the couch.

Now comes the interesting part. Dale's two-year-and-one-hour trip does not seem that way to you. You have been sitting on the couch for much longer. Your hair turned grey and you are now many years older. It's almost as if Dale flew into your future. In fact, the closer the spaceship flew to the speed of light, the faster you aged relative to Dale, i.e. the greater is the difference in your ages. This is so because time slows down when traveling near the speed of light.

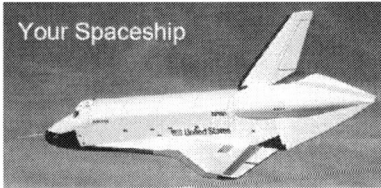
Your Spaceship

Don't you dare now think that you are surprised by what you have just read. You know that this seemingly impossible, perplexing fact is true! You go to the movies, watch television, and read science-fiction. You have seen people travel near the speed of light and learned that time slows down for them there. Nonetheless, this is almost magical, fantastical, nearly unbelievable – and yet many experiments have been done to prove that this really happens. In one test, scientists flew an atomic clock around the world on a fast jet. When it landed, it was compared to an identical clock that had been sitting on the ground. The result was as expected. Time slowed for the clock that flew. Even though they began the day synchronized, after landing, the two clocks no longer agreed. Einstein explained this very real circumstance by changing everyone's understanding of space and time.

For the purist who really wants to know, and don't let that be you, the speed of light is exactly 299,792,458 meters per second. This number has been measured over and over again, and it never varies. Physicists use that number often, and so have come up with a symbol for it. They write 'c,' and among other things, it is used to define the length of the meter. One meter is defined as the distance light travels in $1/299792458$th of a second. More popularly, and less exactly, light travels 186,000 miles per second, about one foot each billionth of a second (nanosecond). That is realllllllly fast! In fact, if you could get a beam of light to orbit the Earth, it would make over seven orbits in one second.

Here, now, is the proof. It takes only a few minutes. It is not hard. At its end, you will then have a "Wow!" at your fingertips.

Go back into your living room. Relax in your easy chair. Watch "Dr. Who" on your HDTV hung on the wall at a comfortable viewing distance of ten feet. We, of course, know you are not really watching as you are currently expanding your mind.

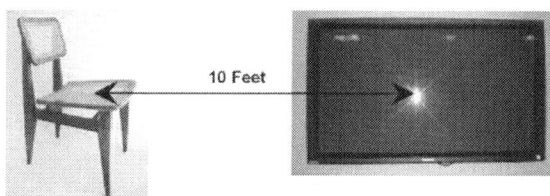

10 Feet

After watching your TV for a while, you decide to exactly duplicate the viewing room on your yacht and watch "Star Trek" on your TV there while traveling 30 mph (of course on the yacht, you're using knots). Later you repeat

Your Yacht

this on your private jet and watch "I Love Lucy" at 600 mph. As long as the TV and chair are 10 feet apart, the time it takes for the picture to reach your eyes does not change. The speed of light for anyone, no matter where they are or how fast they are moving, is always '*c*.'

Even if you were aboard your spaceship as it hurdles through space – no matter how fast it travels – you would still see the picture from the TV travel 10 feet to your eye. If you measured it, it would take the same amount of time.

Pause for a second now and make sure that you agree with everything you have just read. It is all exactly as you expect. There has been nothing unusual or gimmicky. Perhaps you learned something: *The Principle of Relatively* just means that the laws of the Universe are the same in any moving environment – scientists call these environments *frames of reference*. The speed of light onboard your yacht, for example, is the speed of light as it is in any room where you are, no matter what is around that room. So we've now created four frames of reference with identical internal construction: your living room which is not moving; your yacht going 30 mph; your jet going 600 mph; and your spaceship traveling near the speed of light.

Before going on with this tale, remember what the world was like before Einstein, when the rules put forth by Galileo and Newton held all the answers. If Dale was standing by your TV and threw you a basketball (no matter which room Dale was standing in) what would happen? In your living room, the ball flies at 10 mph. In your yacht, it still travels 10 mph relative to what you and

Isaac Newton

Galileo Galilei

Dale see. But someone sitting on the ground and looking through the porthole will see that the ball's speed as *additive*, meaning the ball is traveling 40 mph – the 30 mph that your yacht sails plus the 10 mph the basketball flies (assuming they're going in the same direction). On the jet, the ball travels 610 mph to an outside observer, and so on for the other two rooms. This Galilean, Newtonian world is the world we live in everyday because the speeds we deal with here on Earth don't approach the speed of light. This is what was known before Relativity.

Now, here is the surprise twist to the mystery. You have obviously forgotten that your twin, Dale, has been keeping you company. He (or is it she – don't you know, after all he/she is your twin) has been watching the experiment, over and over again, from the back of each of the rooms (on your yacht, jet, etc.). Dale agrees that no matter what speed the room is moving, the picture's light always travels those 10 feet in the same amount of time.

Dale then goes outside and begins to observe you by looking through the window (or the porthole). He/she holds on tightly to the window (porthole) and travels exactly alongside you as he/she peers through the window. Everything remains exactly the same while Dale moves along with you (is motionless relative to you and the TV and the room). You both still see the same thing. But then Dale lets go and stands on the ground (the street, an Island, a planet...) and watches through the window as you pass by. You, of course remember that Dale has wonderful eyesight, able to see clearly what is happening in the room even when it is speeding past.

You now know that the picture's light takes the same amount of time to reach your eyes no matter where *you* are, so the speed of light is always the same. That is true for Dale, too, even when standing outside. The light seen has only one speed, *c*. So that you are completely clear about this, here it is again. Regardless of whether you're moving at 30 mph, 600 mph, or near the speed of light, its speed is *c*, both for you and also for Dale, whether inside or outside.

How can you and Dale both measure the same beam of light and determine it is traveling at the same speed? There is now only one difference between the two of you. You are moving quickly aboard the spaceship – and Dale is not, and the light from your TV must leave the ship to reach his eye. For him, the light travels further than 10 feet in the amount of time it travels 10 feet for you.

Both your and Dale's observations take place in the same time. You both see the light leave the TV and reach your eye. For each of you, however, the light travels a different distance. Of this there is no doubt; there is absolutely no dispute about the distance each of you measure.

There is left only one way to account for the conundrum – *time* is different for each of you; *time* is slower on your speeding ship than it is for your twin, Dale, standing still on the ground. Although the clock on the wall of your spaceship is running normally to you, and the watch on Dale's wrist is running normally for him/her, you and Dale are experiencing time differently from one another. For Dale, your clock is running slow; for you, Dale's watch is running fast.

That's it. The proof that time slows down as you go faster is simply to describe the two circumstances, the one where moving, and the other, observing the moving situation from a relatively stationary frame of reference.

In both cases, since the speed of light is constant no matter how fast or slow the observer is moving, you can exactly calculate the differential in the speed of time between two frames of reference. It turns out that for the speeds which we encounter in everyday life – driving in a car, or flying in an airplane – the slowdown in time, though real, is so small as to be virtually invisible. Traveling at one-millionth of the speed of light – on a jet airplane, for example – causes time to slow only by a factor of 1.0000000000005. But as you get closer to c, that changes. Traveling at 80% of c makes a 60% difference in time, and this percentage grows rapidly from there.

You may be here expecting more. Remember that the purpose of this chapter is to give you something that many people do not have, a "Wow!" There are many such, and you will acquire others. For now, you can prove that our Universe is different than it had been believed to be for thousands of years by all of humanity. As this book has progressed, you have received things that were somehow missed in your life. Each of them will make your success a little bit easier. If you stop right now, with a proof that only the most educated in the world know, you may have given the first body blow to a horrible specter holding you back from succeeding.

Einstein's Trolley was mentioned earlier. It is real, an old clock tower in Bern, Switzerland. It dominates the center of the town and can be seen for a long distance as you travel on their electrified trolley line. People still look to the huge clock to tell the time. They often use it to set their wristwatches – even while riding the trolley.

Clock Tower in Bern, Switzerland c1900

Einstein wondered what happens when the trolley is traveling near the speed of light. He saw that his wristwatch would keep on ticking, as does the tower's clock seen by passersby. Looking back at the clock, Albert envisioned the clock hands seemingly moving ever more slowly as the trolley's speed increased. At the speed of light the hands would appear to freeze because a new light image would be unable to catch up to the trolley. The insight that time and speed seemed to be related opened a door for Einstein. Speed is related to distance – so time and space became related in his mind.

You now know how to prove one of the most mystical things in the Universe: Space and time are not separate but instead are related and are more accurately written as a single entity, *space-time*. What follows now is very important to realize.

You can prove "that it is so!" You cannot prove "why it is so."

Our Limited Perceptions

Humans can live in temperatures extending from a bit below zero to somewhat over 100 degrees Fahrenheit. Temperature is a measure of how much atoms vibrate and occur at a much greater range. The lowest possible temperature in the Universe (where atoms stop vibrating) is absolute zero. This is 0 K on the Kelvin scale which is equal to −273.15° Celsius and −459.67° Fahrenheit. The highest temperatures in the Universe occur when sub-atomic particles collide and can reach billions of degrees Fahrenheit.

Clearly, humankind exists in what is a very, very small portion of the possible temperatures in the Universe. Our experiences in this tiny realm shape our perceptions and understandings. Although we can measure and probe reality outside this realm with machines and science, we cannot truly appreciate what it is to exist there, no more than we can know what it's like to travel at the speed of light – for now.

The point is, we live in a narrow range with limited knowledge. We live on or near the Earth's surface. No human lives more than two or three miles above sea level (not counting the astronauts on the International Space Station) and none below sea level by some hundreds of feet. Our understanding of this world is thus shaped by where we live. No one lives near the speed of light, so the knowledge of how very different *time* at that speed differs from life at our speed is not known.

The Universe is not strange – it's just sometimes different from how it is seen within our normal range.

Other Parts of Einstein's Universe

While your twin was traveling to that distant star at near the speed of light, if you had measured Dale's height, he/she would have been shorter (though not from his/her perspective). Dale's mass would have similarly increased. In fact, the heavier Dale gets, the more energy it will take to move the spaceship. As Dale approaches the speed of light, he/she becomes infinitely massive which would require an infinite amount of energy to keep the spaceship accelerating.

Even as Dale's spaceship gradually approached the speed of light, he/she would have measured the speed of light to be exactly the same as always. No *matter* can reach the speed of light, so nothing can travel faster than it through space – not stars, not atoms, not you.

Conclusion

You may not be able to explain *why* all the above is so, but you will always, and easily, be able to give the proof that *space-time* is the proper way to write *space* and *time*, for they are inextricably linked.

How smart are you? To see the world as it really is and not as it seems is one mark of the intelligent. To know now something of what you did not know is another.

There is a difference between education and intelligence. Never assume that you can't understand something. If you take the time to understand something, you can learn anything given the proper instruction. Don't underestimate your own innate abilities.

If you found the science discussed in this chapter fascinating or intriguing, learn more. There are many sources of information available to you and many of them are written assuming that you're not already a physicist or engineer.   Wikipedia.org is a fantastic source of scholarly information and it's free. Or you can simply do a search online or in your library for words used in these stories like "speed of light."   Exercise your intelligence; increase your education; do research; learn, because you *are* smart.

EPILOGUE

You have come to the end of this book, so it can't have been an absolute stinker. You have seen a lot and have possibly used some. Stuff from many experts is in the book – it is not theft to learn from them. You may have been amused, shocked, had long-held beliefs questioned or even confirmed.

You saw that all the themes – the *Stuff to Know* – build on one truth:

You have it within you to improve yourself – to *Be More Better!*

The themes were simple, yet powerful: There are always choices and using the experience and perspective of human history makes your decisions better; Forces around you ebb and flow, they are part of the human condition; Giants are real and from their shoulders you can see further; Value the power of knowledge and have faith in your own ability to learn; Your future is still to be written.

You learned some practical skills – *Stuff to Use*. You were shown the essence of some important topics in science and technology and reminded that there is lots of other stuff to aid in your growth. Memorizing it might be useful in making you more knowledgeable, but after having used it, you will be wiser. Wisdom is the difference between knowledge and experience.

You may want to reach out with suggestions as to how to improve this book or with ideas for topics that should be included in the next. There is much which we all need; some was provided here, some is still needed. Those who give, get more in return!

Though this book is ended, your life will **Be More Better.**

ABOUT THE AUTHOR

Michael J. Czuchnicki

Mike's earliest memory is of his father teaching him to read. He spent his summers being guided by his grandmother, on the mined-out Appalachian mountain his grandfather had worked. Back in Brooklyn, he would often help his mother behind the mahogany bar of the family's tavern – child labor laws, or no. His high-school years were spent in an experimental curriculum with all classes taught in Spanish, a precursor to his language hobby, now including Hindi and Mandarin. He has earned two Degrees from Stevens Institute of Technology and spent time at MIT, too.

Mike's career includes the technology offices at the AMEX and AIG; now he consults around the world. He is frequently published, working at the New Jersey home he shares with his Theresa. He tries to both create and give to others and believes this is not his obligation, but his greatest pleasure.

LIST OF IMAGES

Chapter	Figure	Description
Cover	1	Cover Design (Courtesy: J. Milano)
1	2	Xaverian High School, Brooklyn, NY
1	3	Disco Ball (Courtesy: Sarah of Brizzle, UK)
1	4	Footprints in Sand
2	5	Venus
2	6	Sir Isaac Newton
2	7	Blackett Observatory, UK
2	8	Mercury, Venus, Earth, and Mars
3	9	Omar Khayyam
3	10	Albert Einstein, c1947
3	11	Thomas Edison with Phonograph
3	12	Marie Curie, c1911
3	13	Henry Ford, 1919
3	14	Helen Keller, c1904
3	15	Alabama Quarter with Helen Keller
3	16	J. K. Rowling, 2010
4	17	"Speak Better" in Four Languages
4	18	Democratic Convention, Denver, CO, 2008 (Courtesy: zenobia_joy)
4	19	Practicing the Piano
4	20	Staring Eyes
4	21	Seal Performs Trick at Pittsburgh Zoo
4	22	El Diario Vasco Spanish Newspaper
5	23	Royal Flush
5	24	Young Man Reading by Candlelight
5	25	Congressional Medal of Honor
5	26	Children Reading
5	27	Dracula Book Cover
5	28	The Red Badge of Courage Book Cover
5	29	Herman Wouk, 1955
6	30	War and Peace Book Cover
6	31	"ABC" Calligraphy
6	32	Fountain Pen
6	33	Girl Writing
7	34	"Vitruvian Man" by Leonardo da Vinci
7	35	"The Creation of Man" by Michelangelo
7	36	Human Eye
7	37	Idea Light Bulb
7	38	Smiley Face
8	39	Aristotle
8	40	Cuban Flag on Outline of Cuba
8	41	Fidel Castro, 1959
8	42	Dashboard of MGB Roadster

INDEX